TRIALS OF BURMA

MAURICE COLLIS

Trials of Burma

faber and faber

To
Frank Fearnley-Whitttingstall

This edition first published in 2008
by Faber and Faber Ltd
3 Queen Square, London WC1N 3AU

A CIP record for this book is available from the British Library

ISBN 978-0-571-24087-6

'The end and object of human society is to increase in men their sense of duty, one to the other.'—*Civitas Dei*, LIONEL CURTIS.

'The impact of British ideas on Indian society was thus complicated by the opposite and no less powerful influence to which the English were subject in India. They tended to acquire a certain distrust of the principles underlying the society by which they themselves were produced. The policies which appealed to them were such as England could not follow to the end without renouncing the law of her being. The West in adjusting its relations to the East was hampered by the tendency of its representatives to lose their grasp of its own essential ideas.'—*Civitas Dei*, LIONEL CURTIS.

PREFACE

This is a personal history, and I am well aware that to some it may read like the history of a man who thinks he deserved better than he got. I can only say to such readers that my motive in writing it has not been to argue a case of that sort. It so happened that the story told in this book illustrates a conflict of principles—if you like, of opinion—upon whose issue depends our whole philosophy of empire. That such a philosophy matters to us, and matters especially to-day, a book like Mr. Lionel Curtis's *Civitas Dei* abundantly proves. My story (a true story, in every detail) might be read as a concrete illustration of the main argument in that book. It had to be told in the exact and personal manner which I have employed. But I trust that no reader of it will think that I regard myself as its central figure. It was in my experience that these things came to pass. But the hero of the piece, so to speak, is that ideal which few of my readers will wish to disavow—the ideal which the old apologists for empire used to call 'the white man's burden' and which now is conceived as the deliberate transformation of conquests, formerly achieved for purposes of gain, into a commonwealth. That is something which I can only present through the things that happened to me. And if now, after seven years, they still seem to me important enough to put on record, that is not, as I have said, because I am concerned about myself, but because the present state of the world has made me realize the obligation, which rests on anyone who is in a position to do so, to underline the unworthiness and futility of 'smash and grab' in human relations. We have not yet completely grown out of our earlier possessive and domineering view

7

of empire. If this record can help to bring us closer to what I believe to be our right mind, it will have done all that it was written to do.

As I have said, this is a true story in every detail. In relating the prosecution of Messrs. 'Hughes' and 'Mitchell' in Chapter III, and Lieutenant 'Fortescue' in Chapter VII, I have, however, refrained from using the real names of the accused persons. These names are, of course, on public record, but they are irrelevant to the purpose of this book.

Maidenhead,   MAURICE COLLIS
   November 1937.

CONTENTS

9

CHAPTER ONE

1. ALL SOULS

_____

On a raw afternoon in December 1927 Geoffrey Faber
and I set out from London for Oxford. In the suburbs a fog
descended and it grew so thick that I had to stop the car.
Geoffrey got out and walked in front, while I crept after
him in bottom gear. With Oxford fifty miles away and
darkness falling, this was an inadequate method of progression, but we continued doggedly, because to go back
became as difficult as to go on. Our perseverance was re-
warded, for in half an hour the fog thinned and Geoffrey
embarked again. It was still not very safe—once a tree
loomed in front of us and we avoided it by inches—but at
six o'clock we crossed Magdalen Bridge and shortly afterwards drew up at the porch of All Souls College.

The porter told me I was to stay in Lionel Curtis's
rooms. Here was an odd turn, for Lionel Curtis was best
known to members of the Indian Civil Service like myself
as the reputed inventor of Indian Diarchy. For me to go up
casually to Oxford with the Bursar of All Souls and be
allotted the rooms of the man under whose constitution I
had laboured for years gave me a sniff, as it were, of something to come, and as I followed the assistant porter
through the draughty passages, I was sure the coincidence
pointed a sequel.

The rooms themselves were bare enough, as ascetic as a
monk's cell, though a fire had been lit and in a corner
gleamed the blue of some Persian tiles. I changed my
clothes and went down to the Smoking Room.

Faber was waiting for me with a glass of sherry.

11

'As it's Saturday night a good many of the Fellows are dining in,' he said, and added, 'You'll be interested to hear that Simon is coming. I must introduce you to him later on.'

That was it, then; I had felt there was something in the air—for Sir John Simon had just been appointed Chairman of the Parliamentary Commission, which was to visit India and Burma and make recommendations for a form of government more liberal than Lionel Curtis's diarchy.

At dinner I was placed next a Fellow whom I used to know well as an undergraduate at Corpus. He was my year, and after the Honour Schools we had parted, he going on to an academic career in the university, while I had set out for Burma as a Civilian. It was a long time since then—sixteen years. Now in the panelled hall, hung with the portraits of scholars and divines, as I ate my well-cooked dinner, drank from fine glasses good wine, handled the old silver, I was oppressed by the contrast of my own existence, passed on remote sea shores where the wind sighed in the casuarina-trees or beside rivers which flowed through extravagant flowers. Perhaps I had done wrong to choose the active life, perhaps I should never have adventured beyond the cloister and the library.

'You know,' I said turning to my companion, 'I once wanted to be a don.'

'I remember,' he said. ' Wasn't it Shaw-Stewart's year that you sat for the All Souls Fellowship?'

'Yes, I thought seriously then of the university.'

'It might not have suited you; you were such a romantic. There are silences here, you know. You couldn't have borne them.'

'What happened to Shaw-Stewart?'

'He was killed in the war.'

I had been lucky, then, to yield him my place. Had I entered the life of books and contemplation I should have been thrown by a contrary fate into an extreme of action. That I had sailed to Burma had probably saved my life.

'You are going back soon, I suppose?' he asked.

I told him that my leave was nearly up, that I was returning in February.

When dinner was over Geoffrey Faber introduced me to Sir John as an Indian Civilian on leave from Burma.

'Burma, that's Innes, isn't it?' he said in his objective way, naming the Governor, and went on to ask a number of questions.

'We shan't get round there till this time next year,' he concluded. 'Whereabouts will you be then?'

'I can't say, but perhaps we shall meet.'

He turned away to speak to someone else.

2. BESIDE THE IRRAWADDY

A little later I received a letter from the Burma Secretariat in Rangoon to say that on return from leave I was to take charge of the administration of the Sagaing district as Deputy Commissioner. I had been in Sagaing in 1912, and remembered it well as a country town in the heart of Upper Burma. The Irrawaddy went by it and adjacent were the old capitals, Ava and Mandalay. Sagaing, too, had once been a capital, and it had one claim to international interest—Yung-li, the last of the Great Ming, had lived there in 1660, as a fugitive from the Ch'ing. But it was a dead little place, and as I packed up I was by no means thrilled by the prospect ahead of me.

A month later I got out of the train on the eastern bank of the Irrawaddy and looked over the river to the Sagaing shore, a wide prospect in the splendid light. Behind the town with its mat and wooden houses was a cluster of yellow hills, on the top of each a golden pagoda, with monasteries in profusion on their lower slopes.

There, bathed in sunshine, secret and still, was Buddhist Burma. Coming upon it suddenly, after long leave in London, it seemed like a picture in an old book of travels. I was ferried across and soon stood under the tamarinds on the farther bank, speaking with those who had come to meet me.

One enters as through a door into such a life. The door closes behind and after a while one appears never to have been anywhere else. But at first all is strange. Though I had known Burma for so many years, passing through the door was just as strange as ever.

Setting about to get my focus, I found the place was in a state of expectancy. It seemed that an event of moment was impending. There was no secret about it; an official announcement had appeared. Sir Charles Innes, the Governor, was coming to inspect.

'His Excellency will be here on March 14th,' the Commissioner of the Division told me, when I called on him. 'I depend on you to supervise the arrangements.'

I got my focus and threw myself into the work.

The Burmese are masters of the pavilion style of architecture and, as it was a pavilion they had to erect on the river bank for Sir Charles to step into from his boat, a delightful structure soon took shape. It was made of bamboo and coloured paper and was modelled on the main hall of the 'Centre of the Universe', as King Thibaw had called his palace at Mandalay. Laughing and spring-like, it rustled at the water's edge, the spire strung with little flags. There was one trifle about it I did not appreciate. The paper roofs were printed to look like corrugated iron. That useful article had first been introduced by the Public Works department and the Burmese had learnt to use it instead of thatch. It was less inflammable and more lasting —that was how one excused the substitution. But now I perceived that it also had an aesthetic appeal to the Burmese. To do honour to His Excellency the carpenters roofed his pavilion with it, or rather, with a very close copy in paper.

Early on the appointed day everyone was in position, that is to say the officials and their wives, the Municipality and board members. The civil population was conspicuously absent, for the Government of Burma was an official government.

Sir Charles stepped ashore. He was a handsome man, with a very good address. They conducted him to the dais inside the pavilion and there invited him to sit down on the best chair Sagaing could provide—in the Empire style, to the best of my recollection. The President of the Municipality read a loyal address, to which His Excellency listened with a natural urbanity.

Outside, except for a few policemen, there was no-one in sight. The immense river went silently past and the flags on the pavilion flapped jauntily. One was afflicted by a vague sense of disharmony. Sir Charles himself could hardly have regarded the occasion as more than a piece of routine.

That was what diarchy looked like in 1928 in a country place.

Later, in the Commissioner's drawing-room, I was introduced to Sir Charles. His cordial manner permitted me to forget that I was a Civilian more than ten years his junior. In almost a natural atmosphere we conversed as two Englishmen, to the amazement, I thought, of some of the onlookers.

The subject of the Simon Commission happened to crop up. Sir John had already landed in India, had seen the black flag and read 'Simon, go back!'

'Nothing like that could happen in Sagaing,' said I, making conversation.

For a matter of fact it is not the Burmese way to be rude.

The Governor agreed. 'Anyway, he isn't landing here,' he said.

I found something chilling in this remark. Sagaing was such an unimportant little place. Great events were pending; Burma after a long eclipse was going to have her chance; if she could gain London's ear, her life would be changed. That Sir John Simon would not land even for a moment at Sagaing, cut one clean off from the chief interest of the day. Rather forlorn, I continued the conversation.

When it was time for Sir Charles to give someone else an innings he said to me very pleasantly: 'Well, Collis, I hope you'll like your new district.'

I replied: 'Thank you, sir, I'm sure I shall,' but I felt like a man condemned to exile.

I was too sensitive to the stir in the air to want to stay in Sagaing, and, curiously enough, I did not really believe that I should. Yet afterwards, when I considered the matter, when I reflected that the Governor himself did the postings, I did not see what hope there was that I should not stay. Clearly it was his intention that I should, yet from somewhere within me came the assurance that I should not.

3. THE NECROMANCER

With the departure of the Governor I was able to savour the place at leisure. My house was on the bank of the Irrawaddy, which, as the weather became hotter in April, rose higher with the melting of the snows in far Thibet. A scorching wind would be blowing, the soil was hard and cracked, but the river grew stronger and rode freshly through the drought.

By the water's edge old tamarinds threw a massive shade, though their leaves were like lace. Here and there were gold-mohur trees with startling red blossoms, which waxed until each tree was like a flame, a strange sight for eyes accustomed to English landscape.

At dusk I liked to walk on the bank. The blossoms of the gold-mohur had no perfume, but there were other blossoms, and when at this time the wind fell these would sprinkle me with their scents. Across the water was Ava, where the Glass Palace Chronicle had been written. Its walls were split by banyans and tufted with other growths, and behind them in the reflected glow stood up the pinnacles of bat-infested shrines. The place had been deserted for a hundred years, though villages and fields lay within its square, and simple people planted rice where once had been streets.

One late afternoon I went over the river and came to a stubble field inside the rampart. By the side of the field was a summer-house of bamboo and thatch, in which a serious company was seated on mats. They were looking at the field and at some white flags and string lines which enclosed a part of it, wherein an elderly Burman was digging a hole.

I turned to the clerk who accompanied me.

'What is happening there?' I asked.

'It's a necromancer digging for treasure,' he replied, as calm as could be.

'Let's go up and speak to those people in the summer-house,' I said.

The clerk was young, obliging, perhaps over zealous, for he went ahead of me without the circumspection which the occasion demanded, and, while still some yards from the spectators, announced: 'His Honour, the Deputy Commissioner.'

I am alive to atmosphere, and though the men seated and the necromancer bowed I felt sure they were not glad to see me. English officials generally desired to inspect something, to inquire about a crime or to look into a tenure. My arrival must seem extremely inopportune. If I asked questions at such a moment I should certainly be told nothing. So for the time being I made no remark, just looked at the necromancer and his little flags.

When they saw that I was not going to cause trouble they began to talk. The necromancer leaning on his spade volunteered:

'I have secured the ghost and found the bones.'

'What ghost?' I asked.

'The guardian ghost,' he explained. "It can't get through my lines, and as I've found its bones the treasure must be close.'

It began to dawn on me then. Of course, in this old city of Ava much treasure must have been buried; there had been many alarms and many sacks. Royal treasure was always guarded by a ghost, the ghost of a person buried alive on the site, whose soul had been enslaved to watch it for ever.

'Have you seen this ghost much?' I asked an old man on a mat.

'The ghost has been observed,' he said cautiously. 'It has been frequently observed, and if any ordinary person had tried to dig here for the treasure it would have shown its power.'

'How can you be sure there is treasure buried at this very spot?' I asked, stupidly, I fear.

'The ghost walks here,' he said, 'and, besides, the necromancer has found its bones. Treasure is always under bones.'

The necromancer left his trench and came up. He carried a little bone in his hand. It did not look like a human bone, but as I had never handled bones, I said nothing.

'The ground is as hard as a brick,' he told me. 'It may take me days and days to get down to the treasure.'

'You're sure it's there?'

'I always find something in the end,' he replied with a roguish look.

I felt a little disappointed. It was not, I perceived, a genuine case. Evidently the owner of the field had seen a ghost and concluded it was a guardian ghost, thereafter engaging the necromancer to dig. The man was no doubt paid something in advance. He would salt his excavation with an old coin or so.

As I returned home across the river, now so dark that the far shore was invisible, I recalled that I myself had once seen a guardian ghost. I was in Arakan at the time, the north-western seaboard of Burma, and was spending the night in the deserted capital of the Arakanese kings. The rest-house was on the reputed site of their treasury. It was a wooden structure raised on piles, with a wide flight of steps leading up to the veranda. I was seated in a room off the veranda and by the light of an oil lamp could see the steps. Mr. San Shwe Bu, the Arakanese archaeologist, was talking to me. At about nine o'clock I felt the building quiver and sway for a moment. My companion looked up in surprise. 'Like a little earthquake,' he said.

At that instant I dimly saw an old Arakanese woman slowly mounting the steps. It was much too late for anyone to come with a petition and I stared at the woman in some surprise, while she stared back at me from the top step with an intent expression on her wrinkled face. For an appreciable time she regarded me so and then passed out of sight, as if down the veranda, from which there was no exit except into the rooms.

'Somebody's outside,' I exclaimed, jumping up, but I knew that I had seen a ghost, for there is no confusing a ghost with a mortal. It is not your eyes that tell you, but a sense which leaps up suddenly within. We went on to the veranda and searched the rooms. There was nobody there, nor did I expect to find anyone.

Next morning, when some local notabilities came to pay me a call, I said something about it. They looked at me with interest and increased respect. 'Your Honour saw the female ghost bound to this spot by the old kings to guard their treasure,' they explained. 'She is seen mounting the steps and always passes down the veranda.'

'How did the kings bind a spirit?' I asked.

'They buried a person alive at the proper place.'

'Yes, yes, but why should that bind the spirit?'

'At the moment of death the spirit was caught in a magical net.'

'I do not understand.'

'Our old kings understood, as your Honour has seen for yourself.'

'Why did the house shake first?'

'The ghost desired to attract your Honour's attention.

'How did she shake the house?'

'It was not the house she shook, but your Honour's mind.'

As I crossed the dark river to Sagaing the scene of three years before came back to me vividly, and I recounted it to a young Burman magistrate who had joined the boat.

'I don't believe in ghosts,' he said.

That interested me. His degree at the university obliged him perhaps to be superior to the local rustics? But no, he had a practical reason. 'During the war,' he explained, 'I was in the 2nd Battalion of the Burma Rifles, and after the armistice was stationed at Kantara on the Suez Canal. One day at Port Said the Arab mob rose and killed the British A.P.M. and his guard. We were hurried to the spot, and, finding the mob wild and pillaging, fired on them and killed two hundred. It was night and we were obliged to bivouac in the street among the dead bodies. I saw no ghosts,' he added. 'If such things exist surely I should have seen them that night?'

When I reached home the butler had dinner ready for me and I sat down to it like a man who has earned his food. Though my chief, the Commissioner, would not have welcomed a report on what I had seen, I was quite sure that I had not been wasting my time.

4. THE MURDER

Sometimes my routine duties also were not without colour. I remember on Empire Day, the 24th of May, getting up at 5 a.m. The sun had not yet risen over Ava, and the air was washed and cool, though it was the height of the hot weather. Imagine a summer dawn in England, the prelude to a day of great heat, picture a river landscape, early boats, and then intensify the scents and flowers, the light, the silence, and the expectancy. If you can do that you will know what I saw, when I stood on the veranda looking out.

My car was in the porch, and there appeared shortly the Superintendent of Police. We were going out to investigate a murder which had taken place deep in the country. Mr. Fforde was a man who knew Burma well. At no time had he been out of the East, though like many another born in such circumstances he lacked the power of telling what he knew.

A woman called Ma Twé had been murdered. Her home was a village called Shwelingyi (Where Gold Sparkles Much), and it had been reported to us the night before that as she reclined in the cool of dusk on a small platform in her garden a person unknown had killed her with a gun-shot. Our visit amounted to what officially was called 'Visiting the scene of the crime'. The subordinate police had the case in hand already and we should find them on the spot conducting their investigations.

Fifty minutes in the car took us to a village where the

road ended. There two ponies were in readiness, diminutive animals twelve hands high. On these we made our way to the river bank and trotted along it for a couple of miles, till we saw Shwelingyi on the other side. A boat should have been waiting for us at this point, but it was not there, and we were faced with a stream a mile wide. The time was about seven o'clock, for the sun had topped the palm-trees. A strong wind was blowing to us across the river, rustling the high reeds along the grassy bank. There was no-one about, not a soul in sight. We were on the point of turning our ponies, when I caught a glimpse of a canoe deep in the reeds. It was piled with firewood, and sitting in it was an old fisherman and his daughter. I hailed them at once: 'What village are you from?'

The old man came ashore and Fforde told him our predicament. 'The Deputy Commissioner wishes to cross,' he said.

With a fine show of manners the fisherman with his daughter's help unloaded the firewood and placed his boat at our disposal.

'Hold their Honours' ponies,' he said to the girl, 'and wait here while I ferry them across.'

As we put off, balancing in the dugout, I could see the girl with the reins in her hand. She was unused to ponies and nervous at being left alone with two, a pretty girl with a red skirt and wide-open eyes.

We headed into the wind, the fisherman paddling vigorously.

'Did you know Ma Twé, who was shot?' asked Fforde.

'She was a rich woman,' said the fisherman, 'the richest about here. Seated on her mat and talking about her rents, the shot struck her—so I heard, your Honour.'

'Her rents?' said I. 'Was the murderer a tenant?'

But I ought to have known better than to have asked a direct question. The fisherman had not the smallest intention of being drawn into so dangerous a topic. He made no reply and put on a spurt.

It took a good half-hour to reach the other side. We clambered out and I told the fisherman to guide us to the village, which was near by but not visible from where we stood. After two hundred yards we came upon an unexpected arm of the river, on the other side of which on a high bank we could see houses. Here was another obstacle. The water was not more than two feet deep, but as I was wearing a pair of Savile Row jodhpur riding-breeches, I did not want to have them ruined.

'Wade across, will you,' said I to the fisherman, 'and tell them to send us over a cart.'

The old man tucked up his skirt and crossed to the houses. We could hear him shouting: 'The Deputy Commissioner has come.' There were immediate signs of activity. We saw people scurrying about and in a very short time a cart appeared drawn by two bulls. The driver put them at the water and was soon with us.

'How's this?' demanded Fforde. 'Did you get no orders to meet us on the other bank? I sent a constable last night.'

'No orders came,' said the cartman. He appeared abashed.

The truth was, of course, that the orders had come but that the headman had not expected us so early, being unfamiliar with the rate at which cars travel.

We climbed into the cart. A bright red carpet had been spread over the bottom, and seated upon it we crossed to the other side, the cartman holding the bulls' tails in his hands to prevent them swishing us with water.

The headman received us. He was decidedly fussed, and led the way at once to Ma Twé's house. It stood in a compound shaded by knotted tamarinds, a wooden house on eight-foot piles, thatched and with a granary beside it. Under a tamarind was the fatal platform on which Ma Twé had met her death.

'She was sitting on this mat,' said the headman, unfolding a bamboo mat and laying it on the platform, The mat was stained with blood, and as he unrolled it in that way fumes of blood rose up. Fforde leant over the mat and he breathed the fumes. They seemed to stifle him, he could not get his breath.

'Roll it up,' he said, pale and shaken, and turning to me, 'The smell of blood seems to choke me; I have asthma, you know.'

Blood on a mat does not speak to me in that fashion, and the revelation of its power over another, a policeman, too, added greatly for me to the interest of the occasion.

We were standing in a group of rustics, relatives of the dead woman. Under the house a few girls smoked and regarded us sideways. The subordinate police in charge of the investigation had already whispered their suspicions to Fforde; not a tenant, but an heir, was the person suspected. A gun had been found in his house, a gun which, it was said, he had borrowed on the day of the murder. It was a slender thread; no-one had seen him fire, no-one had seen him armed in the village street; or if they had, they were keeping it to themselves.

I had no hope at all that any examination by me of the suspect would advance matters, but feeling I must do something to justify my presence I desired them to produce him. A youth was brought forward.

His eyes rolled and he looked extremely guilty. Or was it that he was embarrassed at being questioned by a white man in poor Burmese with a poorer accent? I could not tell. Frankly, I had no idea whether his statement that he had borrowed the gun to shoot birds was true or not. I soon became convinced that I was wasting my time and also the time of the subordinate police. They would have to ferret round; it would take them weeks to dig out their witnesses and induce them to speak. So, in the best manner I could muster, I told them to get on with it, but my recollection is that the culprit was never found, the village having its own reasons for hushing up the crime.

We again took the cart over the inlet and came to the main river, where the fisherman was waiting with his little canoe. But the headman had prepared a more splendid departure. A large sampan now bobbed at the edge, with mast, sail, and steersman complete. The wind behind us, we shot across the river, dangling the canoe from a rope at our stern. Beyond the reeds the ponies were safely browsing with the reins over their heads and the girl still holding on to them. She looked up with a half-smile, as we landed, as if to say, 'What a job for a lady!'—for slight and graceful, neat and clean, the wind in her red skirt and her black hair coiled up, she looked a lady; and, poor though she was, she took the rupee which I handed to her with an air, and without a sign what the money meant to her.

5. THE ASTROLOGER

Pottering round the villages was all very well, but when June was ushered in with the monsoon storms I became restless. Was I really to stay indefinitely in Sagaing and spend my time, till I went on leave, as a country justice? I could not see myself in that role. Yet with the new season I began to fear that I should have to stay and watch from a distance the important events, which everything told me were on the way.

The pressure by the leaders of political thought in India, which had obliged Whitehall to send out Sir John Simon and his Commission before the end of the ten years' trial prescribed for diarchy, was felt even in rustic Sagaing. In the most picturesque or remote villages, where hitherto life had been an affair of crops and festivals, there began to appear societies, where men talked seriously of passive resistance to the payment of taxes, an order of ideas totally alien to the Burmese temperament. More characteristic of that temperament and equally symptomatic of a charged atmosphere were the antics of a sort of pretender on the district border, a man called Bandaka, who thought, like the Boxers, that he could drive the foreigners out of the country by magic. In the town of Sagaing itself there were even people who believed in his pretensions.

One day news was brought that he had been seen in the vicinity. As a warrant was out for him police were hurried to the spot and the man alleged to be Bandaka was arrested. To make sure the right man had been caught, Mr. Fforde called in certain elders of the town who had known Bandaka a few years previously. They were respectable people of the old school and they sat in a circle and studied their man for some time.

'Well,' said Mr. Fforde at last, 'is he Bandaka or is he not?'

'He does not look like Bandaka,' they replied, 'but it is impossible to say whether he is Bandaka or not, for Bandaka has the power of changing his appearance at will.'

Bandaka was a rustic projection in traditional Burmese form of the growing dissatisfaction felt by everybody for the diarchical constitution. The Sagaing villagers knew that something was brewing, but they could not express themselves in modern phraseology. In advanced Indian circles a Nehru would formulate destructive resolutions; in Sagaing Bandaka planned magically to destroy diarchy. Both men had precisely the same object—a reformed constitution, but Bandaka could not put his aspirations into the current patter, which was as unintelligible to him as his magic was to us. So confused was political thinking in the villages that the term 'diarchy' was taken to be a word of abuse. Thus a man, losing his temper with his wife,would say, 'You are a diarchy', as we might say 'You are a damned fool'.

Popular unrest was intensified by an old prophecy that the years 1930–1 would see some startling events in Burma. As I wandered round the villages in June 1928, listening to all these rumours and imaginations, I became more and more convinced that the subconscious mind of these simple people had caught an echo of something big and alarming.

Wondering what was in the wind, what was to happen to me, I recalled how seven years before I had made the acquaintance of an astrologer in Arakan. I was then Deputy Commissioner of Kyaukpyu, a little port on the Bay of Bengal between Rangoon and Calcutta. My house was within a stone's throw of a pebbly beach upon which sounded day and night a melancholy surge. When the weekly mail-boat had gone the solitude of that forgotten shore was indescribable. No English people lived there except one old man, as lonely and lost as the place itself.

One day my chief clerk told me of a monk who lived outside the town. He was known as the Taung-yin Sayadaw, or Abbot of the Taung-yin monastery, and was a mystic who practised meditation as a way of entry into truth. He had made a study of astrology, added my clerk.

This sounded to me worth following up. I had arrived at one of the most unfrequented spots in Burma. To find there the rare and the strange was surely possible. Astrologers, of course, abounded in the country, but this monk might turn out to be exceptionally gifted.

I told the clerk I should like to consult him. That was the only practical way of getting to close quarters with his astrology. I was sure that he would never succeed in making his methods clear to me, but I could judge his quality empirically by the event. In plain, if what he told me came true it would be very interesting.

'Has your Honour got a *zada*?' inquired the clerk.

A *zada* is a private astrological chart with commentary and supporting calculations, and it so happened that I had *zada*, for only the year before in Mandalay I had met the senior member of the corps of astrologers which in King Thibaw's time had advised the Government, and he had drawn me a *zada*. It was beautifully done on palm leaf, a little work of art. This I sent to the Taung-yin Sayadaw with the request that he would look at it and come to see me in a day or so, when he could tell me his opinion.

At a time appointed he came to my house. From the drawing-room window I saw him approaching, followed by my clerk and by a young novice, who held his parasol. I went to the hall door to receive him. In the hush, as he came forward, I could hear his sandals rasp the path. He was very short, hardly five feet high, and was dressed in a saffron robe, wound on him like a toga; his head was shaved and bare, and he carried an ebony walking stick with an ivory top, on which he leaned as he hobbled up. Bent and frail, he looked an old man, though he was probably not more than fifty. He had a mild, sweet, and retiring expression.

When we were seated in the drawing-room, the novice and my clerk on a mat behind him, I asked him what in general he thought of my horoscope. In reply, he produced from his robe a scroll of paper and said:

'The Supporter of the Religion has a remarkable chart.'

Animated by this good news, I begged him to particularize.

For reply he handed the scroll to my clerk and desired him to read it out. The first part consisted of a commentary on my private life of the previous three years and was true enough. Then followed the statement that I should leave Kyaukpyu for home at a certain date. Thereafter was a progression, in which short notes were given for the next ten years, up to 1930.

When the reading was finished he said: 'I have taken the progression to the year 1930 because it is a turning-point in your life. In that year you will be much in the public eye, and, as I state in the progression, will come into conflict with some persons of your own nation. But in the long run that conflict will do you no harm.'

The year 1930 seemed a great distance away in 1921.

'Can the Master say whether the events foretold take place in this country?' I asked in Burmese.

'They take place in this country.'

At the time I did not attach more importance to the monk's statements than one can attach to matters outside one's comprehension, but prompted by a desire for knowledge I asked him how he knew these things.

He replied: 'In astrology there are the empiric rules of the ancients upon which an intuitive faculty is brought to bear. My method is this. I get up at dawn, and taking a chart work out the positions and their meanings according to the old rules. A number of possibilities emerge, which have to be balanced and interpreted before a definite finding on the particular case can be given. I concentrate my mind, as in the manner before entering meditation, and cause it to dwell on the possibilities. At that juncture a shape or representation (*na-meik*) takes form for me as before some inner eye. The shape is the shape of things to come and I can translate it into words, which I thereupon write down.'

I thanked the Sayadaw for his disquisition, which I followed with difficulty. Shortly afterwards he rose to take his departure. It occurred to me that there might possibly be some question of a fee, but it hardly seemed the moment to raise it. Later on I learned that he never took a fee.

The first test of his prediction came with the date on which he said I should leave Kyaukpyu for home. I left Kyaukpyu on that date for home. Thereafter, for the seven years until I found myself at Sagaing, the progressed predictions all worked out correctly. So, in the June of 1928, I turned up the old scroll to refresh my memory and see exactly what the Sayadaw had said about that year. The entry was very short; it baldly stated that while at first I should suffer a slight set-back, later there would be a move from the place where I was living to a better place. If short, the entry was much to the point. It told me exactly what I wanted to know. But was it true? It might be true, because for seven years the other predictions had been true. But I had no other reason for believing it. How could I believe what I did not understand? And I did not understand astrology or the Sayadaw's procedure. All I could reasonably do was to wait and observe the event. If the Sayadaw was right again—well, it would be a reason to think he might be right about 1930, about the prominence and the conflict foretold for that year.

I had not long to wait. During the last week of June I received a letter from my wife, who was staying at the official hill station, called Maymyo, forty miles away, to say that in conversation with the wife of a Member of Council she had been given a hint—not to let me buy more furniture. Three days later I received official instructions to proceed to Rangoon and there take over the duties of District Magistrate.

I left Sagaing on 9 July, noting the same day in my diary: 'When I heard that my move was to be to Rangoon, as District Magistrate, in which capacity I should have to sit hour after hour upon the bench hearing interminable evidence in complicated cases, my heart sank for a moment and I wondered if I could do it. But when I reflected on the position of the chief magistrate of the capital, on the great opportunities it would Afford me for acquiring information about that cosmopolitan city, on the amenities for my family and the openings for the future, I became cheerful, and leave Sagaing with thankfulness. I hope never again to walk along the banks of the vast and lonely river under the heavy red flowers of the gold-mohur trees.'

CHAPTER TWO

1. DISTRICT MAGISTRATE

The railroad from Sagaing to Rangoon traverses the heart of rural Burma. From the carriage window I could see that the ploughing was finished. Each rice-field was an embanked pond of churned soil and water. The young seedlings were like pale grass in the nurseries, whence girls chanting old songs would soon transplant them to the fields. Buffaloes, lazing to their necks in wallows, paid no attention to the train; others, ridden by naked boys along the embankments, raised their heads and stared, reflected in the watery landscape, until with a toss of their horns they lumbered away.

Night fell at last. There was no moon. One might as well have been in any land where the wind was soft and warm. I was soon asleep.

The District Magistrate's house was in the garden city of Rangoon called Golden Valley. It had three large bed-rooms and sitting-rooms, with verandas, a tennis court, flowers and a view of the Shwedagon Pagoda. My office was in the city. The road to it skirted the royal lakes, a shaded avenue with the lake water glimmering on the left, while on the right was the maze of shrines, alleys, and monasteries which clustered round the foot of the pagoda, hill. Farther down, the scene became more modern. You saw the zoo and the war memorial, and passing the large chummery where the numerous English assistants of the firm of Steel Brothers were quartered, you crossed the railway bridge and entered the rectangular layout of the city itself. The first street was Soolay Pagoda Road, the cinema and restaurant quarter, the Soolay Pagoda itself dominating the end of it, surrounded by palms and glittering in the sun. My office was not far from the bridge, down Montgomery Street, in a leased building facing the Roman Catholic Cathedral.

Though generally known as the District Magistrate I was officially the Deputy Commissioner of the Rangoon Town District. As such I was not a judicial officer working under the High Court, but an executive officer, exercising magisterial functions, who was subordinate to the Commissioner of Pegu, one of the most important executive officers in Burma. In this respect Rangoon differed from Calcutta, where the Chief Magistrate was a judicial officer.

A judicial officer gets on the bench, tries his cases, and goes home. His work is reported on by the High Court, which inspects his office and takes appeals from his decisions. But though my cases went on appeal to the High Court the Commissioner of Pegu reported on me to the Government. Moreover, my day was not over when I had given judgement in the last case on my file, because, as Deputy Commissioner, I had a general responsibility in the town and my duty was to be fully informed of what was going on, so that I could report to and advise the Government.

I was not responsible, however, for law and order. That was in the hands of the Commissioner of Police. I was a sort of colleague of his, able in emergency to amplify his powers but not competent to give him or his force any orders. Thus it was the sole duty of the Commissioner of Police to prevent breaches of the peace, such as riots, and to suppress them, if they occurred. In such a situation I might have to ascertain the cause of the riots and submit a report with recommendations; I might even have to give the police the statutory authority to fire on the mob; but I was not to direct any action.

In normal circumstances, therefore, my duties as Deputy

Commissioner were loosely defined and light. My real work was to dispose, as District Magistrate, of the criminal cases which came before me. As the senior magistrate of the capital city of a province in the Indian Empire I had the assistance of six stipendiary magistrates, all Burmese, and of two honorary benches. Together we coped with all offences committed in Rangoon and brought to trial under the Code or under local enactments. In the ordinary way it was hack-work, and that is why my heart sank at first when I heard of the appointment. In the districts my duties had been varied and interspersed with touring, but in Rangoon in the normal course I had day by day a long file of dull cases, burglary, wounding, and cheating being the commonest.

Not long after my arrival a Mr. Merrikin was made Commissioner of Police. His appointment was more interesting than mine. As the direct executive authority in Rangoon he was fully informed through his staff of detectives and agents of everything which happened. Politics, the Press, gambling dens, drink licences—all were his affair. He had no need for any advice from me, and, in fact, had he desired advice, I was in no position to give it, as my sources of information were inferior to his. But in any case he did not want me as a colleague in that sense. What he wanted was my assistance on the bench, that I should convict the people he sent up for trial. As far as he was concerned the ideal district magistrate was the man who not only made no excursions off his bench, but who on his bench recorded the findings which were expected of him. Not that Mr. Merrikin was anything but an honest man. When he sent up a case, he intended it to be tried fairly and according to law. But when a magistrate is also, an executive officer, in practice it means that the executive expects a finger in the administration of the law.

All this became clear to me shortly after my arrival. I was to be a sort of recording machine, which, set in motion, turned accused persons into convicts. It was a melancholy discovery for a person who was anxious to apply his mind freshly to the problems of his work.

But had I known what was in store I need not have repined. I was mistaken in thinking that my bench-work must be routine. Cases quite out of the ordinary were to crowd on me and I was to be confronted with the necessity of being first a magistrate and then an executive officer. Obliged by my view that the law had a quality beyond convenience, I should have to take my own way regardless of the Commissioner of Police and at the risk of offending the whole executive. Indeed, so delicate was to become my position that there were to be times when I should look back and wish I was only the machine which in normal times I should have been.

2. THE CHINESE

Before events began to march I had time to look round and see what manner of place I was in. It was very different from rustic Sagaing, which found the modern world so confusing. A cosmopolitan city, where all sorts of people lived, it had a Burmese appearance with its pagodas and characteristic roofs, but besides the Burmese town class it contained large foreign communities like the Chinese and the Indian, while aloof and all-powerful were the English residents ranged in their clubs and occupying the most important appointments.

My position enabled me to explore the town with facility and I took advantage of it, for to see nobody but my own countrymen appeared to me a gross stupidity. The educated Burmese, Indian, and Chinese were very friendly, and an acquaintance with some of them enabled me quickly to form a picture of the Rangoon of the period and so, later on, to see things in perspective.

I remember one afternoon, soon after my arrival, that Mr. Chan Chor Khine, a Chinaman who owned much house property in the city, called for me in his car. It had been arranged that he would take me to see the palatial residence of Mr. Lim Ching Hsong, who had died some years previously.

Mr. Lim Ching Hsong's life was a supreme example of what could be achieved by a poor Chinese immigrant into Burma through industry and force of character. He had become a millionaire rice merchant, and though an attempt to corner the market had eventually done him no good, in his day he was a great figure in Rangoon.

When he became rich, though he had had neither the time nor the opportunity of acquiring taste, he ardently desired to make some show of cultivation. Accordingly, instead of spending his money on coarse pleasures, he built himself a palace, the interior of which he sought to beautify. He decided that he could not achieve the demonstration he desired by a collection of objects to be had in Burma and so, on a tour which he made to England at that time, he purchased show-cases and suites of furniture at the emporiums of Tottenham Court Road, and, on trips to various watering-places, amassed a quantity of commercial pottery decorated with crests and domestic inscriptions. These articles would give an air to his rooms. But something more was wanted; the walls were bare.

He was lunching one day in the Chinese restaurant off Piccadilly Circus when it occurred to him to ask the proprietor, who was a friend of his, whether he knew of any artists who would come out to Burma and paint his walls.

The proprietor immediately drew his attention to a couple of people, a man and a woman, seated not far away at a table.

'Who are they?' asked Mr. Lim Ching Hsong.

'They're young artists, married,' replied the proprietor, 'and from what I've heard, they're good artists.'

'But would they come out to Burma, do you think?'

Mr. Lim Ching Hsong's wealth had not made him proud.

'They're poor,' the other assured him, 'and when they know about your palace it will all seem like a fairy-tale.'

Mr. Lim Ching Hsong was delighted. An introduction was effected. The artists gave their names as Ernest and Dod Proctor, and in due course sailed for Burma.

So much Mr. Chan Chor Khine told me as we drove towards the palace, not in the terms I have chosen, but in the more agreeable manner for which he was known. The visit of the Proctors had taken place thirteen years previously, and as they had become famous during the interval I was eager to see what their early work was like and how it would look in such an unusual setting.

When the palace came into view I beheld a great central tower with wings, the whole roofed with green tiles, figured at the corners in the Chinese manner. We were received in the high porch by Mr. Lim Ching Hsong's youngest son, who had inherited all his father's good nature. With a charming pride he showed me round, calling upon me to admire the contents of the cabinets, the mugs from Brighton with their inscriptions, the little knick-knacks from Clacton and Southsea. The ground floor consisted of seven halls and we went through these, examining the exhibits. In some of the cabinets was modern Chinese porcelain and in others the brass work which is called 'Benares'. When I saw no sign of the Proctors' work, I became uneasy, and at last said:

'Your father engaged English artists to paint frescoes for him, did he not?'

'They are on the first floor,' he replied, and led me to a grand staircase, at the foot of which was the first object of art I had seen, a stone elephant amusingly carved. We mounted the staircase and came to the frescoes.

I must say that they showed no sign whatever of the future eminence of the Proctors. Chinese landscapes of a traditional type, they were pretty and had a technical facility. But where was the artist who had risen to dominate the Academy with 'Morning'? I was disappointed, and when Mr. Chan Chor Khine whispered that he proposed now to take me to the Chinese temple near the docks the suggestion sounded delightful. For all that, the visit had been interesting. Had Mr. Lim Ching Hsong persevered, he might have graduated from Tottenham Court Road to St. James's, and from mementoes of Margate to Crown Derby, or, grounded solidly on his carved elephant, have filled his cabinets with K'ang Hsi and jade. And if his taste had been uncultivated, it was advanced when one thought of the dark barracks in which some of the rich Indian merchants lived, or of the farmhouse simplicity of the rich Burmese. He had been the first Asiatic in Rangoon to live in a cosmopolitan interior. The time was coming when all the upper class, Burmese, Chinese, and Indian, would live in that way.

At the entrance of the Chinese temple we were met by the trustees, who had been warned of our coming. I was conducted through a courtyard to the main altar, on which was a figure of Kwan-yin, the Compassionate Mother. The architecture, which was a great roof on pillars, and the appointments, bronze vessels and lacquer tables, were in the immemorial style, though none of the objects was antique. But the materials used were good and well-made copies can be remarkably convincing, as every collector knows to his cost. Had Mr. Lim Ching Hsong confined himself to such a scheme of decoration, his house might have been in better taste, but it would have been less revealing, a period house without hint of the future.

My attention was drawn to a bamboo tube, which the oldest trustee was holding towards me. In the tube were some fifty thin rods pointing upwards.

'Will your Honour take the omens,' he suggested, smiling.

I was instructed in the use of the tube. I should shake it vigorously before the altar, they said, still retaining its vertical position, and one of the rods would rise up from the rest and, toppling over, fall on the floor. From that it would be possible to read the omen.

I did not understand how a rod could rise up against gravity, but I shook vigorously and awaited the event. Sure enough, one of the rods began to rise. The trustees invited me by signs to persevere, and I continued to shake the tube in front of Kwan-yin. The stick rose and rose until the end of it was free of the tube and it fell to the ground. When they had observed the angle of the compass to which the stick pointed, they picked it up. On it was written a reference number, which enabled them to search a book for the response indicated. When the reference was found, they looked pleased.

'May I inquire the result?' I asked.

'"The steel will become gold", are the words,' they replied. 'Your Honour will certainly rise very high.'

Though human enough to be pleased that their omen was favourable, I was still more impressed by their exquisite politeness. Not content with displaying to me their temple, the trustees had organized its resources of divination to flatter me. How much more delicate was this way than a direct compliment!

3. THE PRINCESS

O n another occasion chance allowed me a peep behind the scenes of Burmese life. One morning towards the end of 1928 I was sitting at home in my study when a car drove up to the door and a Burmese woman got out. I went into the hall to receive her.

'I am Ma Lat,' she said in English, a perfect English without trace of an accent.

Ma Lat—I had not seen her before, but I knew of her, of course. She was the Princess Teik Tin Ma Lat of Limbin, the Middle Princess or second daughter of the Limbin Prince, who had been King Thibaw's brother. When the British took Mandalay in 1885, King Thibaw was exiled to a remote spot in the Bombay Presidency and, later, the Limbin Prince to Allahabad. Ma Lat was in her 'teens when the Crown Prince of Germany visited India before the war. It is related that he was introduced to her at a party in the Allahabad club of which her father was a member, and that afterwards he used to say that she was the most striking woman he had met on his eastern tour. She became engaged to be married about that time to the heir-apparent of Nepal—a love match it was said but—the story goes that the Brahmin hierarchy of Nepal set their faces against the marriage because Ma Lat was a Buddhist. The heir-apparent died, it was alleged, by poison.

After the war the Prince of Limbin was allowed to return to Burma. Besides Ma Lat, he had two other daughters and a son. They found the place much changed. The dynasty, Mandalay, the court were nearly forgotten. The Burmese took no interest in the remnant of the royal family. The aspirations of the upper class were now for a modern form of government, the talk being all of what sort

of a constitution Parliament could be induced to grant.
The country people, whose approach to such matters was
astrological, believed that the mandate of the old dynasty
was exhausted and that the new king—for that was the
way they translated the constitutional change which was
pending—would be of a different stock.

So it was that the princesses, charming, accomplished and
accustomed to the best society in Allahabad, found themselves nonentities in their own country. English officials
were too cautious to encourage them and the poor girls
fitted in nowhere. They lived with their father in a house
called Radana Theinga—one of the old classical names of
the dead capital—and made friends as best they could.

That was as much as I knew of Ma Lat. I took her into
the drawing-room, wondering what it was that had brought
her to see me.

She sat down on the sofa, a beautiful woman, in a blue
silk skirt and a jacket of white lawn, her complexion corn-
coloured, her eyes large and brilliant, and with exquisite
hands. As she seemed a little diffident in beginning, I
offered her some refreshment. At last she said:

'I have come to see you in your capacity as registrar.'

One of my minor offices was that of Registrar of Births,
Deaths, and Marriages. I should have guessed her errand
then, but I was slow.

'As registrar,' I repeated. 'Yes?'

'I'm going to get married, and I want you to perform
the ceremony.'

'Certainly,' I replied. 'May I ask, are you marrying
a——?'

'No,' she said, 'I'm marrying an Englishman.'

'If you will give me the particulars——'

'Herbert Bellamy.'

Mr. Bellamy was a bookmaker.

The marriage of the Princess Ma Lat of Limbin to Mr.
Bellamy aroused little interest in Rangoon. The day was

fixed, 19 October. Normally civil marriages were performed in my office, but on this occasion I arranged to go to the Prince's house.

There were not many guests and Mr. Merrikin, the Commissioner of Police, was the only high official present. Mr. and Mrs. Manook were doing the honours, Manook, the Armenian, whom King Thibaw had employed, and whose wife is known to readers of *The Lacquer Lady* as Selah. Hardly a Bunnan of any position was to be seen. I took my seat at a table at the end of an upper room. The guests were arranged on chairs in front of me, leaving a passage to a door on the veranda. At 4.48 p.m.—the moment selected by the astrologers—the princess was seen approaching through the door, accompanied by her younger sister and the Prince of Limbin. She was dressed reminiscently of the court of Mandalay in a royal *htamein* of oyster-coloured silk set with silver diamanté; her hair, in the loose tail-style, was charged with orchids and there were pearls winding on her throat and breast. She came forward slowly, waving a white fan, with a look of dignity and emotion on her face. Mr. Bellamy followed in a morning coat.

The ceremony of civil marriage is exceedingly bald, for it consists of hardly more than the taking of oaths. When some documents are signed it is all over. On that occasion its abruptness seemed almost rude. I declared them married and took Ma Lat's hand. The occasion seemed to me strange and disturbing. Had the rape of Mandalay ended in this?

4. SIR JOHN ARRIVES

Three months passed and at half-past four in the afternoon of 29 January 1929 the S.S. *Tairea* with the Simon

Commission on board berthed in front of the Soolay
Pagoda. We all went down to the wharf, the entire
diarchical Government, except Sir Charles Innes, who was
waiting in Government House. There were the two Members
of Council for the Reserved Side, the two Ministers for the
Transferred Side, the two Financial Commissioners, my
chief, the Commissioner of Pegu, Mr. Booth Gravely, who
took precedence over all other officials present, a number
of heads of departments, such as the Excise Commissioner—
and Mr. Merrikin and myself. We lined up facing the
ship in our black morning coats and white topees, sweating
profusely, though the weather for Rangoon was tolerably
cool, say 75 degrees in the shade. As Sir John Simon
looked over the rail he could see the whole thing which
he had come to abolish neatly arranged on the wharf-side,
like a stack of files on an office desk.

He was soon climbing down the gangway and we were
presented to him by Mr. Booth Gravely. During his tour
of India he had had presented to him a whole series of
diarchical governments and, though he was exceedingly
polite and it was a pleasure to see a distinguished Englishman in Rangoon, one could not help feeling that we had
only a paper existence for him—and he had had such a lot
of paper in his life!

A reporter of the *Rangoon Gazette* dared to ask him
whether he had a message for Burma.

'We are looking forward with the greatest eagerness',
he replied mechanically, 'to all we can hear and see in your
country.'

He then entered a staff car which was waiting for him
and was driven straight to Government House.

In the course of the next day I received an invitation
from Mr. Auzam, a wealthy Indian, to a garden party in
his grounds on 5 February. Sir John Simon and his colleagues were to be the guests of honour.

At the time appointed I presented myself at Mr.

Auzam's gate. He was a Mohammedan and his wife was English. Rangoon was full of little paradoxes of that sort. There will be a mixed crowd here to-day, I thought, and saying something polite to Mrs. Auzam, I strolled down to the tea tables, arranged by the lakeside in the shade of trees. A cool wind was fluttering the table-cloths. I sat down and was immediately interrogated by two Indian members of the Rangoon Bar.

'Do you think Simon will recommend the separation of Burma from India?' they began.

'I'm certain of it,' I replied.

'Why?' they asked.

'Because all the evidence he will hear in Burma, except that given by Indians, will favour separation.'

'Well, I was told something to-day, which should make the Burmans think before they separate from India,' said one of the lawyers.

'What was that?' I asked.

'The Government will first get Sir John to agree to separation and then they will say that Burmans are not as advanced as the Indians.'

'Well?'

'And so can't be given as advanced a constitution as India.'

'Don't you believe it,' I said. 'The Government would never play a dirty trick like that on the Burmans.'

'It wouldn't be a dirty trick,' said both the Indian lawyers. 'The Burmans have nothing like our brains, and if they insist on separating from India how are they going to run a modern constitution by themselves? They couldn't do it. It would be useless giving it to them.'

There was something about this conversation I did not like, and I got up. At another table near by I saw a senior member of my own service. He beckoned me over.

'Have you been examined by the Commission?'

'No,' I said. 'I'm not on the list of witnesses, not

important enough. By the way, what has the Government been telling Sir John?'

'Separation, of course. The country's solid for it.'

'But what about the constitution to follow?'

'Oh, that!' he smiled. 'As long as the Burmans get separation they won't care what sort of a constitution they're given. It's the Indians they can't stand, not the present form of government.'

'I wonder. But tell me, would you really recommend for Burma after separation a constitution less advanced than India gets?'

'What's the Government to do?' he complained. 'The Burman isn't fit for a regular constitution. How can they recommend such a thing? It's not safe.'

'But the Burmans will go off with a bang if they hear this. It's writing them down as inferior to the Indians. And they're bound to hear about it; you can't keep it secret.'

'The Government is making no secret of it. In their written statement to the Commission they are recommending separation and a certain type of constitution.'

I was completely nonplussed by this. It seemed so rash to tell the Burman to his face that he was not the equal of the Indian, on whom he had always looked down. My companion saw I was shocked and changed his tone.

'Look here,' said he, 'put yourself in the Government's place. How could it seriously recommend a big jump? There will be advance all right, but a steady advance. For all anybody knows, the Indians may get no more than that.'

'The advance is not the point,' I replied warmly; 'it's the slight.'

'You're pro-Burman,' he said, laughing to soften the accusation, though the Burmans were subjects of the same king as he and I.

'I'm pro-Burma,' I retorted. 'I've worked here for sixteen years and I don't want to see the place written down as a backward hole and have a bust up because it is.'

Luckily some more people arrived at this moment and the subject was changed to a discussion of the temperature.

After a good tea I started to stroll round the lawns. The guests had all arrived, but there was a good deal of coming and going between tables, friends calling to each other with animation, while covert glances were directed towards the Commission, which was seated at a large table with some senior officials. Burmans were not much in evidence; one saw them here and there in their bright silks, but the party was not intended to display them before Sir John. At the extremity of the crowd I came across one of my magistrates, a Bunnan who often gave me information.

'Burmese glad to see Sir John?' I asked.

'They're not sure whether they can get his ear, sir.'

'What nonsense! Isn't he examining everyone and anyone?'

'Yes, but the Government has the first say and they can say it so much better. I hear some of the Burmans have got a fright and are now against separation.'

'What do you mean?'

'Well, they think it safer to hold hands with the Indians.'

'But they really want separation?'

'Yes, sir.'

Rumour had evidently gone round already. The Indians in Burma were bound to be delighted, as they did not fancy being cut off from their homeland, but what would be the outcome of so confused a situation? It was no affair of mine, I reflected. My business was to keep on trying my cases. But I was wrong there. In various ways the tension would invade my court-room; I was fated to feel it in all my work.

By the time I had found another seat the sun was setting and that most enchanting of all Burmese hours was descending upon the garden. The breeze was coming in little airs from the lake and on a bamboo stage set with flowers a

Burmese girl was dancing. She was dressed, as Ma Lat had been, in the costume of the Mandalay court, and her songs and gestures raised a ghost of the old days. She pounced and sang, and though her art was gay and whimsical, behind it was all the national aspiration. For the common people it represented the life which had been taken from them, when their country was conquered, and they pictured a free Burma in terms of such a stage representation. For the Burmese guests at the party the dancer was a symbol which animated their resolution to win Burma for the Burmans.

Sir John and his colleagues were watching the girl dance. As a lawyer he cannot have been accustomed to evidence given in this way, but in fact the girl was expressing everything which he had come to Burma to find out.

5. LOST AT SEA

The Simon Commission remained ten more days, and on 15 February embarked for Madras. Their report was to be delayed for another sixteen months. Following their departure Gandhi went to prison, but in Burma, though apprehension and rumour, as we knew later, spread underground, the outward scene was not unpeaceful.

I was on my bench every morning at eleven o'clock. The work was generally monotonous. There appeared to be no end to cheating and embezzlement; the same sort of burglars and roughs were always coming up for sentence. I began to know the evidence before it was given and could tell a false case by the answer to the first question. After tea I often played golf or tennis, went to one of the clubs, and later dined with friends. It was an unintelligent and humdrum existence, but the life of a Civilian at a provincial capital is generally of that sort.

All through the hot weather and rains of 1929 I can remember only one case with any colour in it, and as it brought to the surface some fundamentals of the Burma scene I shall describe it.

One night Captain Dewhurst of the mail-boat *Aronda* reported by wireless that a few hours out of Rangoon that afternoon his chief officer had sighted an open boat flying a flag. He had altered his course and presently hove to with the boat under his counter. On the thwarts were fourteen Indian seamen. He took them on board, and after they had been given food and water he began to question them. The leading seaman was a Serang and he stated that he and his men were the survivors of the tug *Ngatsein*, which had sunk early that morning at the head of the bay.

'Who else was on board?' asked Captain Dewhurst.

The Serang replied that there had been three other persons, the captain, Mr. Pinnington, the chief engineer, Mr. Phillips, and a Madrasie servant of the latter, called Arokiaswamy.

'Where are they now?' asked Captain Dewhurst.

'I don't know,' said the Serang.

By dint of cross-examination the captain elicited that the *Ngatsein*, miles away in the Gulf of Sittang, had sprung a leak and suddenly foundered, when the Serang and the crew had got into the boat. Captain Pinnington, Mr. Phillips, and Arokiaswamy had jumped into the water. The Serang had failed to pick them up. The tide and the waves had prevented him, he said. Captain Dewhurst thought the story very peculiar and said so in his wireless report.

That same night Captain Russell, master of the *Shwedagon*, was navigating his ship towards the mouth of the Rangoon river when he heard a cry in the darkness. It came from the sea, which was dead calm. He stopped the ship and ordered out a boat. After a prolonged search a man was found clinging to a plank. He was brought on board. It was Arokiaswamy, Mr. Phillips's black servant. He had been in the water for thirteen hours and was terribly exhausted.

On examination later by Captain Russell he said that the tug *Ngatsein* had been proceeding from Moulmein to Rangoon. It had anchored the night previous to the catastrophe, as Captain Pinnington was out of his reckoning. Dawn broke with a heavy sea. Soon after a course had been set, one of the native engineers came on deck and reported that water was flooding into the engine-room from the after-hold through the propeller shaft apertures in the bulkhead. There was evidently a serious leak in the after-hold. The pumps were set to work, all hands bailing, but the water rose and the tug began to settle by the stern. When the crew saw that their efforts to stem the inflow of water were fruitless they clung to each other, praying and weeping, whereupon Captain Pinnington ordered them to put on their life-belts and cut the lashings of the lifeboat. They had hardly done so when the tug sank stern first, the lifeboat floating off a few moments beforehand. Some of the crew were in it and the rest jumped into the sea. Captain Pinnington and Mr. Phillips were the last to jump. 'I was one of those in the water,' continued Arokiaswamy. 'I had no lifebelt but saw a piece of wood floating by and clung to it. Those of the crew not already in the lifeboat now climbed into it, but the captain and my master were farther away and we could not reach it. The captain called for the boat to be brought, but the Serang, though he heard and saw, rowed deliberately away.'

Arokiaswamy concluded by saying that after a time he became separated from his officers. All day long, with the sun beating on him, he battled with the sea, his thirst increasing. When darkness fell he gave up hope, for he knew that he could not hold on to his plank all night. But he thanked God he was a Christian or else God would not have heard his prayers.

Captain Russell immediately reported this story to the authorities, and in due course a Marine Court of Inquiry was set up, of which I was appointed president, the two members of the court being Captain Gilbert and Captain Wiles. The Serang and his crew were arrested, bail being allowed. During the ensuing days we examined the parties. Arokiaswamy was in the box for hours. He was a small black man of no apparent physique, but was evidently very much tougher than he looked. Few Englishmen could hold on to a plank for thirteen hours in a tropical sea, with a tropical sun blazing overhead. He stuck to his story that the Serang had deliberately left him and the two Englishmen to drown, though in making that statement, he said, he was running a grave risk, for the Serang had threatened, if he did so, to make an end of him. I pressed him to say whether he could assign a motive. Serangs do not, as a rule, desert their officers. Had there been any unpleasantness on board the tug between Captain Pinnington and his crew? There had been none, he assured me, the Serang had no excuse; he and his crew were Mohammedans. No further explanation was necessary.

The seamen in the dock unquestionably looked a low lot, but they were Chittagonians, and Chittagonians are notorious for their unprepossessing appearance. As a race they do not, I suppose, breed more rascals than any other, but they look as if they did, and that is a grave disadvantage in a dock. When the Serang was asked why he did not pick up his officers he stated that the current carried him away, and when it was pointed out that the same current, to begin with at least, must have been carrying the officers along with him, he lapsed into silence.

The court might have been obliged to decide between his word and that of Arokiaswamy had it not been that there was one independent witness, or fairly independent witness, called Abdul. He had been the captain's servant, had jumped into the sea as the tug sank, and had been pulled into the boat by the Serang. He deposed that the Serang did not row away but looked unavailingly among the waves for the swimming officers. Unfortunately Abdul was also a Chittagonian, and, though he had been the captain's servant, it was possible that ties of blood were for him stronger than loyalty to his late employer and that he thought it less important to avenge him than to save his compatriots.

My two assessors and I spent a long time considering our finding. How were we to interpret the evidence? Was it really true that the Serang had rowed away? Arokias-wamy was a stout little fellow, but he did not like Moham-medans, and thirteen hours on a plank in extreme peril of his life had altogether soured him against them. It was also possible he might have been mistaken. A plank in a rough sea is not the perfect coign of vantage from which to judge nicely of the behaviour of men in a boat.

At last there seemed to us only one interpretation which fitted all the facts. The Serang and his men before getting into the lifeboat were crying with fright. In the boat their predicament must have appeared almost as desperate, for they were a long distance from the coast, the direction of which they could only judge by the sun and to which with adverse currents and winds it might be impossible to row, particularly as the lifeboat was not provisioned. Their plight so overwhelmed them that, instead of searching for their officers, they fell to prayer. As best they could, on their knees, with their eyes closed, bending their heads to the boards they chanted their supplications, oblivious of shouts for help, their thoughts on Allah, the Compas-sionate.

So we acquitted the Serang of maliciously leaving Captain Pinnington and Mr. Phillips to perish, but on the ground that he should have postponed his prayers until he had rescued his officers, nor have importuned God for the succour he was unready himself to give, we directed that he be tried for his ineptitudes under a section of the Indian Shipping Act, which deals with such occasions. I believe a very lenient sentence was eventually passed.

This case, carried in as it were upon the wind of the great bay, was so charged with the colour of England, so rich with our best, that it heartened me like a song. More than any people our bones are on the floor of distant seas; we have a taste for the farther gulfs, a technique in remote dying. Pinnington and Phillips were obscure men, their vessel was only a tug, but they saw first to their native crew before they thought of themselves. With economy of gesture they followed the English way, and when death overtook them had given their testimony.

CHAPTER THREE

1. RANGOON SOCIETY

———————————

In 1929 Burma was governed by the English. Under the diarchical constitution of 1919 the people's representatives had been given certain powers, but in practice those powers were largely advisory. The two Ministers of the Transferred Side, who represented the legislature, might make proposals, but unless the Governor, aided by his two Members of Council for the Reserved Side, gave his consent, they could not pass into law.

The Governor and his Council of Two looked to Rangoon society. From it they derived the opinion necessary for the formulation of their policy.

Now, Rangoon society was wholly English and it was composed of the members of three great clubs, the. Pegu, the Boat, and the Gymkhana. Nobody but a European could be elected to these clubs. Wealth or attainments or character was irrelevant; only race counted. Thus, Mr. Lim Ching Hsong's palace and frescoes, his money and good nature did not excuse the fact that he was Chinese. Neither her royal blood nor her beautiful face could qualify the Princess Ma Lat. The two Burmese Ministers of the Transferred Side were not eligible, nor were the Burmese judges of the High Court of Judicature. Mr. Auzam might give a garden party and entertain the Simon Commission, but if he had had the hardihood to get himself put up he would certainly have been black-balled. Even the Japanese consul was as much an outsider as the rest. All the battleships of his country could not have secured his election to the Pegu Club.

There were three main classes of Englishmen in the clubs, Government officials, officers of the British or Indian Army, and merchants.

The officials were mostly persons like myself who had had long experience of all parts of Burma. We knew the Burmese language, we had spent years in remote stations and had belonged to clubs which were not exclusive. I myself had been a member, for instance, of the club at Akyab, which is now one of the air-stations on the London – Melbourne route. There were quite a number of Englishmen there and the club was in no way dependent for its existence on outside support, as was sometimes the case with smaller clubs in less important centres. Certain of the Arakanese gentlemen and their wives, however, were honorary members, were invited to dinner parties, and joined in all social amusements. We found that their presence made the club more pleasant, for they were dignified and unassuming people.

I have seldom met an English official who did not speak up for the Burmese. It was one of our commonplaces to call them the most engaging people in the Empire. Some of us had Burmese friends to whom we were sincerely attached.

Sooner or later, when we came on transfer to Rangoon, we found that the Burmese were excluded from Rangoon society. To some of us it was a relief to be in a purely English atmosphere again. You could say what you liked; it was more comfortable; all foreigners are rather exhausting. But to others this easy line was too unintelligent. We knew that if we cut ourselves off from social contact with the local inhabitants our work would suffer. In the year 1929 it was not possible for an official to refuse to mix with Orientals on equal terms and at the same time to be good at his job.

Why, then, did we not press for the election of suitable Burmans to membership of the clubs? The reason was that neither military nor mercantile opinion approved, so that, even if all officials had voted in favour of such a step, there were not enough of them to ensure the election of the Burmans they proposed.

The attitude of the soldiers and merchants was easy to understand. If officials had many reasons, both professional and sentimental, for wishing to see Burmans in society, the merchants had few and the soldiers had none. I am speaking generally; among both merchants and soldiers there were individuals who were far too intelligent to live happily in a narrow coterie. But the average man's idea of relaxation after work has nothing to do with improving his mind. It is only necessary to realize what sort of business the merchants transacted in order to see their point of view. Their work lay with Indian brokers and middlemen, people who in no circumstances had any claim to social consideration. They did not meet the Burmese, for that race had little or no share in Rangoon commerce. They could make their fortunes without knowing a word of Burmese and without the smallest knowledge of Burmese history or religion. Some of them were not as ignorant as all that, because certain firms had branches up-country, where they extracted timber from the forests. But broadly speaking there was no immediate business reason for meeting socially the upper-class Burmese of Rangoon. As I have said, exceptional men existed, who realized the importance of the constitutional changes which were pending, and knew how to be in close touch with Burmese opinion, but in a general view the mercantile community restricted its circle of friends to the European members of the clubs, and so were badly informed of what was going on.

British military officers had still less motive for taking the trouble to explore beyond their own class. They were specialists in a matter which did not touch Burmese life at all and if they passed three years in Burma without addressing a word to a Burman, that made no difference to their efficiency. Here again there were individuals who had a keen desire for a wider knowledge and experience, and who were as well informed about things Burmese as it was possible to be after a short stay, but for the ordinary officer who spent the day training his men it would have been unspeakably tedious, when he got to his club, to have been obliged to mix with people other than his own countrymen.

So, in effect, the mercantile community and the soldiers asked that they should not be bothered with the Burmese. It was very human, a very understandable weakness, but it followed that their prejudices remained unmellowed by experience. The English, of course, are not the only people with national prejudices. Everybody by nature dislikes foreigners. Orientals, for instance, have found Europeans very dreadful. During the eighteenth century in China visitors from the West were known as the Red Woollies. Their skin reddened by the sun and their comparative hairiness appeared disgusting to the mandarins. Obliged by circumstances to make their closer acquaintance, the Chinese found they had good hearts. It was discovered that a European, in spite of his barbarous appearance, was after all a human being. But the traders and soldiers of Rangoon, under no necessity of pursuing an acquaintance with the native inhabitants, remained darkly in their prejudices and firmly held the Burmese to be an inferior race.

The public attitude of the Governor on this matter supplies an interesting commentary. The members of the three clubs were on the Government House list and they received invitations, according to their importance, to dinner, lunch, or garden parties. Now, Burmese, Indian, and Chinese men and women were also invited to such functions and it sometimes happened that a military officer would find himself placed beside an Oriental. Manners would come to his rescue and the encounter would pass off; he might even find that his neighbour was pleasant enough. But nothing prompted him to follow the Governor's example. It was assumed that for reasons of political expediency such people had to be invited to Government House and that the Governor had no desire for his condescension to be interpreted otherwise. Some officials in my time were bold enough to invite Orientals of birth and education to dinner in their houses, but they could not do as the Governor did and invite everybody and anybody to meet them. If they were casual in the selection of their other guests the success of their party was in grave danger. I have noticed the expression of charming bewilderment which comes over the face of a pretty Englishwoman as she enters a drawing-room with her husband on such an occasion. 'Who on earth, George, are these extraordinary people?' No official exposed himself a second time to such ridicule.

2. THE SERVANT

One of the last houses in the suburbs, before you entered the streets of Rangoon, was the chummery in which lived the assistants of that important firm of merchants, Steel Brothers Ltd. The assistants were young men from England, most of whom had not been in Burma for long. Every morning at nine they went down to the office and rarely were home before half-past six. That is a very long day in a tropical climate. The young fellows tried to get what amusement they could at the clubs between seven and eight-thirty, at which hour they dined together at their mess in the chummery. On Saturday afternoon they played golf or tennis, and danced afterwards at the Gymkhana Club.

This urban existence concealed from them a great deal which a young man soon learns in a country place. After two years Burma was hardly more familiar than it had been for them as boys at home in England. They lived as English a life as possible against this Oriental background. Provided the background did not advance upon them, they were safe enough; but occasionally it did advance with alarming results.

On 4 November 1929 one of these assistants of Steel's, a Mr. Hughes by name,[1] returned home to the chummery at a quarter to seven. He had been worrying all day about a pair of sleeve-links, which he believed his Burmese servant had stolen. The man was called Ba Chit and had been with him for a year. At first he had seemed quick and willing, but latterly had become less satisfactory. Hughes had begun to miss articles of his wardrobe. Some of his suits had disappeared and now his sleeve-links had gone, links to which he attached a sentimental value because they had been given to him by someone he was fond of.

That very morning he had searched Ba Chit's room. The chummery servants did not sleep in the building. They had their own quarters in the grounds. With his friend, Mr. Mitchell, and Sam, the Indian butler who looked after the messing in the common dining-hall, he had gone to Ba Chit's lodging and turned out his boxes. Ba Chit looked on, as did his wife, who nursed an infant. There had been no trace of the suits nor of the links, but Sam had found some Chinese pawn tickets, which seemed to refer to clothing. And there had been another find, though the significance of it was not clear at once. In a tin they had come upon an ounce or so of something black, and soft as putty. It had a peculiar smell, a smell of poppies.

'What's that?' they had asked Sam.

'Opium, sir.'

Ba Chit took opium, then? Did he steal so as to have money for opium? They knew Burmans were not allowed

[1] As I have stated in the Preface, the names 'Hughes and Mitchell' are not the real names of the two men concerned.

by law to smoke opium. That one's servant was an opium addict was a disturbing fact.

'Sam,' Hughes had said, 'I've got to hurry down to the office now. I'm late already. Will you take these pawn tickets and find out whether they refer to my clothes. If they do, get the clothes back. And about the links, bring Ba Chit to my room when I get home this evening. I'm certain he has the links somewhere and I'll make him tell me.'

Mr. Hughes had his usual long tiring day in the heat, and the moment he was back in the chummery he sent for Sam, who appeared shortly with a bundle of clothes. He had been the round of the pawnshops during the afternoon. Hughes identified the clothes as his own.

'Now go and call Ba Chit,' he said. 'I must get those links out of him somehow or other.'

All this sounds straightforward enough, but Hughes had just given an order which in result was to set the whole town by the ears.

Sam did as he was told, went down to the servants' quarters and told Ba Chit his master wanted to see him at once. Ba Chit's wife, a young woman called Ma Kywé, watched her husband go. As she knew he was guilty of theft, she felt apprehensive and, taking the baby with her, went out and stationed herself under Hughes's window, which was on the second floor of the chummery, thirty feet above her head. Some of the other servants joined her there.

For a while they waited, looking up from time to time at the lighted window. It was now quite dark, a warm night without a moon. A constant flow of cars passed the gate of the chummery compound. The lights of the cinema quarter over the railway bridge were reflected in the sky.

At about half-past seven Ma Kywé thought she heard a cry coming from the room where her husband was being questioned.

'What's going on?' she asked the others. 'Are they beating him, do you think?'

It was impossible to say. She became alarmed. Her husband had been in the room a long time.

Again they waited and then, abruptly, repeated cries sounded from the room. Violently agitated, Ma Kywé exclaimed: 'The master is killing my husband, I know it!' and began screaming loudly: 'Ba Chit is dying, he is being beaten to death!'

She now distinctly heard her husband's voice. He seemed to be answering her.

The crowd under the window increased. Presently the Indian night-watchman was seen approaching.

'The master has sent me out—you're to stop that row and get away,' he said angrily to her in his language.

She retreated a distance, but, when the watchman had gone, returned to her position beneath the window. It was now past eight o'clock. Should she go into the building and try to find out what was going on? She dared not, as the wives of servants were not allowed in the chummery.

Then something dreadful happened. A body dropped from the window to the ground.

They all stared. Lying almost at their feet was Ba Chit on his back. Ma Kywé shrieked and raised him in her arms. She called him by name, but he did not answer.

A few minutes later Hughes and Mitchell came running round the side of the house. They went up to Ba Chit and bent over him. 'Get a car, quick!' they directed. 'We must take him to hospital.'

Another assistant called Adamson shortly arrived with the car. They lifted Ba Chit, who was dying, on to the seat. Hughes, Mitchell, and Ma Kywé then got in, and they drove off. Ma Kywé was weeping, but before they reached the hospital she said to Mr. Adamson, who understood Burmese: 'If Ba Chit was a thief he deserved some punishment, but to be beaten the way they beat him was too much.'

Mr. Adamson did not press her to explain her meaning.

At the hospital Ba Chit was handed over to the doctors. He died that night without recovering consciousness.

On the way back from the hospital Hughes stopped at the police station and made a report. 'I was questioning Ba Chit about his thefts when he suddenly threw himself out of the window,' he stated. Ma Kywé remained in the car. She neither went into the hospital nor the police station. When they reached the chummery it was after nine-thirty. Hughes had had no dinner; he was tired and shaken. As they all got out of the car Ma Kywé broke the silence which she had preserved since her remonstrance to Mr. Adamson.

'I am going out of this,' she said to Hughes, with the extreme acrimony which an angry Burmese girl can put into her words, 'but before I go I want the month's wages due to my husband.'

It was the 4th of November and the October wages had not yet been paid. Ma Kywé's demand was translated to Hughes by one of those present, and it appeared unwarrantable to him. His servant Ba Chit had turned out a rascal, who had stolen his suits, stolen his sleeve-links. The mere fact that he was dying or was dead was no reason why his wife should expect money which if he were alive would certainly not be paid. The links were worth more than the wages. He would not pay. Why should he pay? The woman's manner was outrageous. She did not seem to realize the depravity of her husband's character, a thief, an opium addict, and now a suicide.

'Say that I owe her nothing,' he announced. When this was conveyed to Ma Kywé, for a moment she was astonished. Then indignation overcoming her, she said harshly: 'Keep your wages, then!' and disappeared into the darkness.

3. SIR CHARLES PROSECUTES

—————

The next day, when she knew that her husband was dead, Ma Kywé went to the police station. 'I have a complaint to lodge,' she told the Burman officer in charge. 'The master sent for my husband to his room. He was there for over an hour and I heard his cries as they beat him. His body then fell from the window. I want the police to investigate what happened in that room. Perhaps murder was done in it.'

The officer made a note of her statement, but said: 'Your master has already reported the matter. While Ba Chit was being questioned about his thefts he threw himself from the window.'

'But why should he kill himself? The thefts were trifling. Something was done to him in the room.'

'We shall make inquiries,' replied the officer vaguely and sent her away.

Ma Kywé left the police station feeling that nothing would be done. Hughes was a white man; the Government was a white government; what chance had she, a penniless Burman woman, she argued, of obtaining an impartial investigation? Hughes's word would be taken and no-one would think any more about the matter.

In the ordinary course an inquest was held over the body of Ba Chit. The coroner was a Burman, one of the city magistrates subordinate to me. He used his discretion, called what witnesses he thought proper, and found that Ba Chit had committed suicide. The circumstances in which this had taken place he did not seek wholly to unravel. As soon as the evidence established suicide he brought in his verdict.

During the following days the story of Ba Chit's death

spread among the Burmese. It was whispered that Ma
Kywé had accused Hughes of murdering her husband; it
was said that Hughes, having beaten Ba Chit until he
collapsed and was dying, had thrown him out of the window to avoid the inconvenience of a corpse on his hands.
These allegations were repeated far beyond the confines
of Rangoon and came to the notice of political societies
the members of which already regarded the Government
with the gravest suspicion. These persons seized at once
upon the affair as evidence of what they had always
alleged—that there was one law for the white and another
for the brown—and declared that the Government had
ordered the police to burk the case, as it was impossible to
let a prosecution go forward against an employee of so
important a British firm as Steel Brothers.

Great popular indignation was aroused by these statements and members of the legislature drafted questions to
be asked at the coming session of the House. The coroner's
verdict was brushed aside as the finding of a subordinate
official who did not dare to offend authority.

Meanwhile the police had been investigating the case
in the ordinary way. They examined all the witnesses they
could find, but there seemed no section of the code under
which Hughes could be prosecuted. The Commissioner of
Police, realizing that the matter was of importance, as
public interest was so much engaged, made a special report
to the Government.

When the papers were put up, to Sir Charles Innes he
perceived at once that it was desirable to bring Hughes to
trial. If a case was not brought there would be no vent for
the feelings which had been growing in intensity, but with
Hughes in the dock everything there was to be said could
be said, and if he was innocent the magistrate would publicly declare him so with the fullest reasons, when popular
excitement would subside. But under what section could
he be tried? In consultation with his judicial secretary Sir

Charles hit upon S. 330, by which any person who caused hurt to another with intent to extort a confession or compel him to restore property could be punished. There was some evidence to show that Hughes had struck his servant to induce him to restore the sleeve-links or to say where they were hidden. S. 330, it was true, had been framed to prevent the police torturing suspects, but there was no reason why it should not be invoked in this case. Accordingly Sir Charles sent the judicial secretary privately to the Commissioner of Police with a message saying that a prosecution under S. 330 was desirable.

On 25 November, three weeks after the death of Ba Chit, Hughes was arrested. He was brought before me and I granted him bail. Then began a trial which at the time was regarded as sensational and which in its bearing upon what happened in 1930 was a highly significant event. Sir Charles was right. The country did benefit from the trial. But for two individuals it was not pleasant—for Hughes because he was a scapegoat in a matter which passed far beyond his own actions, for me because to give a decision where conflicting emotions are deeply aroused always invites much criticism.

4. THE TRIAL

The trial was fixed to begin on 19 November. I left home about ten o'clock, on my way down passing the chummery, at which I looked curiously. One could see the window from which Ba Chit had fallen.

As my court was only a temporary residence pending the erection of a fine court-house overlooking the river, it had an indifferent aspect. The court-room itself had been used before as a showroom for the sale of cars, and with its glass shop windows fronting the pavement it still had that appearance. A side door, from which stairs led up to my chamber, opened on a yard where I used to leave my car. I drew up there as usual that morning and an Indian *chaprassie*, a wonderful old figure redolent of the days described by Kipling, salaamed and carried my case-boxes upstairs.

My chamber, a modest room, commanded a view up Montgomery Street towards the railway bridge. A few people were waiting to see me and I disposed of their applications. At eleven o'clock my Burmese bench-clerk entered to announce that the parties in the Hughes case were ready below. With the case-file in my hand, I went downstairs, entered the court-room and mounted the bench.

I was about to call on the Public Prosecutor, U Kyaw U, to open the case, when a Burmese barrister, a Mr. Paw Tun (who is now Minister of Home Affairs), rose in his place at the bar and said:

'Your Worship, I am instructed by my client, Ma Kywé, to file a complaint charging Messrs. Hughes and Mitchell with the murder of her late husband, Ba Chit.'

Saying these words, he handed up to me a typed and stamped complaint.

There was dead silence at this unexpected move. Hughes, who was seated below me waiting for the Public Prosecutor to open on the minor charge, was alarmed to find that he had now to meet a charge of murder. He consulted hurriedly with his counsel, Mr. Darwood, a barrister who had held the appointment of Sessions Judge at Moulmein in 1920, where I was a magistrate subordinate to him.

Mr. Darwood: 'I submit that as the police found no substance in Ma Kywé's complaint, your Worship may be pleased to dismiss it, after recording her statement.'

The court: 'I am bound to proceed in the ordinary way, Mr. Darwood. If she shows ground, I must examine her witnesses.'

Mr. Darwood: 'As your Worship pleases.'

What had happened was clear enough. Ma Kywé, having failed to get the police to send Hughes for trial on the charge of murdering Ba Chit, had brought a direct complaint to me, as she was entitled to do under the law, and as she had been advised to do by some of the political leaders. She was represented by a first-class lawyer, whose fees, perhaps, had been guaranteed by those Burmese associations which regarded her case as of national importance. She stood there, young and determined, in her white muslin jacket and red silk skirt, but I noticed at the back of the court a number of grim females wearing coarse grey homespun. I had never seen Burmese women so unbecomingly dressed. They were the extreme left wing of the political front and it was clear that they had come to see that Ma Kywé got justice.

I now asked her to step into the box and take the oath. My clerk placed in her hand an oblong parcel of palm-leaf manuscript bound in red cloth. Holding this level with her forehead she took the oath, saying 'May I die the deaths named in this palm-leaf, if I do not speak the whole truth.'

Mr. Paw Tun then examined her. She described in detail how she had stood under the window, heard her husband's cries, seen him fall thirty feet to the ground. 'There is only one explanation', she exclaimed, 'of these facts. For his thefts of to cause him to return the sleeve-links the two Englishmen, Hughes and Mitchell, beat him, and finding that they had gone too far, that my husband was dying, flung him from the window in an effort to cover their misdeeds.'

It was clear that Ma Kywé's allegations were not impossible and that I must give her an opportunity of proving her case. Therefore I addressed the bar, saying that in the circumstances I would first take up the murder charge and desire Ma Kywé to produce her witnesses. Afterwards, if necessary, I could proceed with the police prosecution. I then turned to Mr. Mitchell, who was in court, and asked him whether he understood that he was charged with murder jointly with his friend. He replied that he understood and asked for time to engage a lawyer. Accordingly I directed that the case should stand adjourned until 10 December, to give the two young men ample time to prepare their defence. Bail was allowed.

On 10 December I reached the court-house rather earlier than usual and noticed a crowd at the door. Monks in their yellow robes and women in homespun jackets were pushing to get in. The court-room was not large and there were insufficient seats for such a number. My clerks were attempting to regulate the crush. Preference for seats was being given to the monks. I found this spectacle very disturbing. That the case had aroused public interest I knew, but I did not realize, until I saw the monks, the excitement which prevailed. The best class of monks never attended trials. The men I saw were political monks, members of secret societies, half-educated, rude fellows, with a great authority over the lower classes. Rough and overbearing, they were shuffling into the court-house, supported by the peculiar-looking women in homespun. These people represented old-fashioned Burma, the Burma of Bandaka, the magical bandit, the Burma which believed in the coming of a deliverer-king.

No Englishmen seemed to have come to see Hughes and Mitchell tried, but they could count on much English sympathy. I knew that members of the Gymkhana Club had made it clear over their drinks that they considered the Government prosecution quite needless. When they heard that Ma Kywé had brought a complaint of murder their indignation was great. The Government was accused of weakness. Had no prosecution been launched on the minor charge Ma Kywé and her rascally supporters would never have come forward with the major charge. If Hughes had beaten his servant the fellow deserved it, no doubt. It was unfortunate that he should have jumped out of the window,

but was Hughes to be blamed for that? Obviously
not; Ba Chit was a neurotic. 'Encourage the Burmans and
you see what happens,' had said a gentleman at the Boat
Club. 'The Government means well, no doubt, a fair trial
and all that, but just look what you have—a false charge of
murder and every Jack Burman in the place getting up on
his hind legs. It's all nonsense. I hold no brief, mind you,
for Hughes and Mitchell. Those two young fellows, like all
young fellows, have a lot to learn. But to have them tried
like criminals is madness. What's it all for, I should like
to know?'

As I took my seat on the bench Mr. McDonnell, the
best-known criminal lawyer in Rangoon at that time, rose
at the bar and said that, supported by his learned friend,
Mr. Darwood, he was representing Messrs. Hughes and
Mitchell. With Mr. McDonnell appearing in that way the
case had become a *cause célèbre*. He was a remarkable
man, with a large following in the clubs, at one or other of
which he might be found any evening, the centre of a listening circle. He was famous for his stare, into which he
could put more righteous surprise than any man I've ever
met. Some people found it extremely intimidating and it
was worth a great deal of money to him. His firm advised
the mercantile community in all legal matters, and as his
general outlook coincided with theirs it has already been
adequately described.

The examination of Ma Kywé's witnesses occupied two
days, but they were able to throw no light on the affair. Not
one of them knew what had happened in the room. They had
all heard cries, swore that they had heard blows, and had
seen Ba Chit fall. Murder they deduced from the circumstances, but it was my duty, not theirs, to make deductions.

The evidence of the police surgeon was of more importance. He had conducted a post-mortem examination of the
corpse and had found no trace of beating upon it. All the
injuries had been caused by the fall from the window.

The question I had to decide at that stage was whether a *prima facie* case of murder had been made out. If I thought there was even a possibility that Hughes and Mitchell were guilty, it was my duty to commit them for trial before a jury in the sessions division of the High Court. There had been as yet no cross-examination, no defence. Counsel had reserved both. The only clue to what might have happened in the room had been provided by Hughes himself in a statement not under oath. He had declared that when he began to question Ba Chit the servant seemed to lose his nerve and lay on the floor shrieking. The questioning was continued, and he flung himself from the window.

I was, however, not concerned at that time to discover in detail what had happened in the room, but to decide whether there was any, even the smallest, probability of a conviction in the Sessions Court.

On the face of it Ma Kywé's story was not inherently improbable. If one were walking down a street and observed a crowd of people looking up at a window, from which issued the sound of blows and cries for help, if these sounds continued and were followed after some time by the spectacle of a body falling from the window, one might legitimately conclude that there had been foul play. But an important difference existed in the present case. The house was occupied by a number of Englishmen, who admittedly had no part in the affair, whatever its nature, and they had heard nothing. Moreover, the servants who alleged that they had heard beating and cries had not called the attention of their masters to what was happening. I concluded that if there were cries they were not caused by beating, the sounds of which had either been imagined by the servants or invented by them. The medical evidence supported this view. That left me with cries and a fall, and no evidence.

On 13 December I summed up in that sense, and, after discharging the two Englishmen, added: 'Whatever may have happened in Mr. Hughes's room, it was not murder.

Whether Mr. Hughes maltreated Ba Chit or not; what were the circumstances of that maltreatment, if any; why Ba Chit threw himself from the window; what may be the connection between that desperate act and the treatment he received; what criminal liability must be borne by Mr. Hughes—all these are questions to be resolved in the police prosecution now pending against him.'

My ruling was calmly received by the monks and ill-favoured women. It took me half an hour to deliver, and as it was in English and the monks did not understand that language, they were no more informed of my reasons at the end than at the beginning of it. But they understood enough to know that the order was one of discharge, and it may be that the care with which I had tried the case reassured them or that they themselves, having heard the evidence, recognized its weakness, for there was no expression of anger or disappointment on their harsh faces as they departed, nor after they had obtained a translation of my orders was anything more heard of the murder story.

Next morning my order appeared verbatim in the newspapers and was eagerly read by all the Europeans. When I dropped into the Pegu Club that evening I was received with acclamation. The bar was crowded with officials and the managers of the big firms, and I was soon the centre of a group, which congratulated me on the way in which I had saved two Englishmen from a wrongful accusation. The wording of my judgement and the clear manner in which I had put the case for the prosecution and then destroyed it by ridicule was warmly applauded.

For a time I basked in this sunshine and accepted the drinks which were lavishly offered, but when I heard them declare that Hughes was a wholly innocent man I became uneasy. The police prosecution was still pending and I was not yet sure what he had done. That he had done something seemed probable, for otherwise there would not have been such a feeling against him. The Burmese servant class was noted for the easy terras on which it lived with its masters. I felt that there was still much to come out and began to find congratulations, which pinned me down to a point of view, very embarrassing.

That night I went to some entertainment in the Jubilee Hall, a building by the old race-course, where balls and concerts were given. When it was over and I was getting into my car, which was parked outside the railings, I noticed that the car next to mine contained Mr. Booth Gravely, the Commissioner of Pegu. When he saw me, he remarked: 'Well done, Collis. Keep it up in the other case.'

Some men might have been pleased by such a remark, cordially made by their chief, but coming after what had been said in the club it alarmed and shocked me. It shocked me because it suggested that I was assumed to be in some kind of a racket; it alarmed me because I now saw clearly what I was expected to do by authority and I did not know whether I could do it.

5. THE CHARGE OF TORTURE

On the Monday the police case began. Had Hughes tortured his servant to compel him to restore the stolen links? To answer that question I should have to find out in detail what had happened in the room.

It soon appeared that there were only two people who could give any information on that point. These were the two persons who were with Hughes at the time, namely Sam, the butler, and Mitchell. Neither of these men was an independent witness, particularly Mitchell, who had been the co-accused in the murder charge, but as there was no-body else I was obliged to found my view upon their

Statements, which, in point of fact, supplied a coherent narrative not inconsistent with the rest of the evidence.

What they said came to this: Ba Chit was a temperamental youth, who had fallen into the opium habit. When he reached Hughes's sitting-room he knew that his thefts had been proved, for Sam had retrieved his master's clothes from the pawnshops by means of the tickets found in his room. After the clothes had been checked in his presence, he was asked about the links. Where were they? They must be produced or the police would be summoned. Hughes did not know Burmese, but with the help of Mitchell, who had come in, Ba Chit was urged to answer the question — 'Where are the links?'

He would not answer. Perhaps he could not answer, if the links had been melted down. The two Englishmen seated themselves in chairs with their backs to the window. Ba Chit stood in front of them. 'Where are the links?' 'Go and get the links!' 'It will be the worse for you if you do not get them!'

Ba Chit could not circumvent the point by pretending not to understand, for they were now addressing him in Burmese. 'Get the links!' 'Go on, you shall get them!'

This pressure continued for half an hour, when he suddenly collapsed on the ground. 'Get up, it's no good your pretending; get up at once!' Hughes, much irritated by what he thought was a further attempt at evasion, leaned forward and boxed his servant's ears.

Ba Chit got up, his nerve completely gone. He began to wail and ask for pardon and to blubber. 'It is no use going on like that! Shut up! We want the links! Now go and get them!' They pressed him in this way without intermission for another half-hour.

'It seemed the only thing to do,' explained Mitchell. 'We thought he was evading us, holding out, refusing to give the links.'

'But he had asked pardon,' I interposed.

'Yes, but we wanted the links.'

'As he admitted his guilt, why did you not hand him over to the police and let them get the links?'

'We thought that we were more likely to be successful than they.'

Ba Chit by this time was looking ghastly. He fell to the floor again and began screaming hysterically. Hughes again leaned forward from his chair and boxed his ears, shouting, 'Get up, I tell you! You can't fool us with that!'

Ba Chit lay there moaning, grovelling, begging for mercy.

'Where are the links? Go and get the links!'

He suddenly stood up and turned into the bedroom. The two Englishmen congratulated themselves. He was going at last to get the links. But he emerged again from the bedroom, crouched past them, and flung himself out of the window.

Such was the account given by Mitchell, and it struck me as close to the literal truth. The two youths had had to do with a neurotic. They had failed to realize his condition, and by persisting in their questions and demands had driven him to suicide. There had been no beating beyond a couple of boxes on the ear, given to induce him to take a hold of himself. No hurt within the meaning of the law had been inflicted to force him to restore property. The hurt which had been inflicted was not of a material kind. Nor had there been criminal intention. Hughes was innocent of the charge.

The arguments of counsel took place on the Tuesday. The Public Prosecutor had little to say. He was aware that the charge could not stand, but pointed out that under the Code it was not permissible, strictly speaking, for a master to box his servant's ears. Hughes had committed that technical offence and he could be charged therewith at the discretion of the court.

As the speech of the Public Prosecutor tailed off, Mr. McDonnell rose with a well-calculated air of indulgence on his face, 'May it please your Worship,' he began. 'I am delighted to perceive that the case against my client, which began with all the rigour of a murder charge, and which developed thereafter into a charge of torture, an offence of sufficient seriousness, for it is punishable with seven years' rigorous imprisonment without the option of a fine, has wilted away under the rays of truth until now we are concerned only with a box on the ears.'

After a pause to allow the subdued merriment which greeted this effective opening to die away, learned counsel proceeded to speak of his young client's difficulties. We all knew what a bad servant was like. While happily in Burma it was the rule for masters and servants to live together with mutual esteem, there were occasionally exceptions. His client, with only a short experience of the country, had, he feared, been unwise in his choice of Ba Chit as a valet. But how was a young man, fresh from the healthy atmosphere of an English home, to know the way to cope with an Oriental drug addict? When questioned about the property he had stolen Ba Chit had behaved like a lunatic. What more natural than that, disgusted at such an unmanly spectacle, his client should have boxed his ears in an effort to get him to pull himself together? Surely one was entitled to exercise a certain amount of control over one's servants, and if that control was reasonable how could anyone, particularly a young gentleman not long from a public school, be supposed to foresee that the servant would jump out of the window?

When Mr. McDonnell sat down, so persuasive had been his manner that my first impulse was to discharge Hughes without further ado. Had I done so it would have saved a great deal of trouble. In a short order I could have shown that the prosecution launched against him at the instance of the Governor had no substance and, without further remark, have directed his release. There was every inducement to take that course. The unpopularity of the prosecution with the mercantile community and their friends has been mentioned, and though the Burmans had been greatly pleased by Sir Charles's initiative Burmese opinion was of small practical account at that date and was, in any case, largely satisfied by a very full trial lasting a fortnight.

But though, as I say, inclined to be rid of the affair, I had the uncomfortable feeling that to close the case without an attempt to show it in a wider light would be to decline to use the authority entrusted to me as District Magistrate of Rangoon. As long as I was District Magistrate my duty was, so I conceived, to express myself freely on the facts before me. If the District Magistrate did not say what he thought, the Government and the people of Rangoon were defrauded. They had created and were paying for an appointment the incumbent of which was supposed to up- hold British justice in its widest sense. If he declined the responsibility of speaking his mind he would be no better than a subordinate at half his salary. To explain the case fully involved accounting for the Burmans' indignation. A colourless discharge would suggest that I did not under- stand that indignation or wrote it down wholly to error or prejudice.

But I did understand the Burmese indignation and was inclined to think that it must be shared in part by some Englishmen. It was impossible to blink the fact that after an interview with his master a servant had committed suicide. There were reasons—the man was neurotic, his nerves had been frayed by drug-taking, though there was no evidence to prove him a regular drug addict; and he knew that he was a thief. But why had his cross-examina- tion been so prolonged? Why, when it should have been clear that he was in no state to answer questions, was he still questioned? And was the recovery of a pair of sleeve- links so urgent a matter that it justified such pressure? The answer to these questions appeared to be that Mr. Hughes did not know what he was doing, and that he did not know what he was doing because he had insufficient feeling for his servant, who was a Burman. Had his servant been English something might have prompted him to stop his questions before the catastrophe. The sentiment that one man has for another of his own race would have told him when he was going too far. That no hint of the kind reached his intelligence suggested to me that he did not feel himself to stand in a human relation to Ba Chit. The fault was certainly not his alone; the society in which he lived was at least partly responsible.

That he did not see his servant as a fellow-being was further shown by his insensibility in the face of death and the bereavement wrought by death. Irritation and anger may cause a man to lose his sensibility, but in general the sight of death will bring him again to a more pitiful mood. Had Hughes's servant been English, when he leant over the crumpled body and saw the young wife's anguish instinct would surely have prevented him refusing her claim for her husband's wages. But, as it was, the wife was just a Burmese girl, asking for money to which she had no right. His heart was not touched. And this was, at any rate partly, the reason why the Burmese thought him a mur-derer—because he seemed to them callous, as only a murderer could be callous.

These reflections passed through my mind and counter-acted Mr. McDonnell's indulgent argument. I told him that orders were reserved and the case adjourned until Friday the 20th.

During the two days at my disposal I wrote the judge-ment, which ran to five thousand words. I felt obliged to make an exhaustive analysis of the evidence so as to banish for ever from the minds of Burmese critics the suspicion that Hughes had committed a criminal offence. When I had made that clear beyond question, and had discharged him, I added something of the opinions which I have expressed above.

On the Friday morning the judgement was duly delivered, and on the Saturday it was given in the morning newspapers, in which it occupied four columns and a half. That afternoon Sir Charles Innes was leaving Rangoon for a tour in Upper Burma, and, as usual, senior officials went to the station to see him off. When I arrived on the platform I saw Mr. Lloyd[1] the Chief Secretary, in conversation with Mr. Booth Gravely. I went up to them and something was said immediately about the case.

'What did you think of the judgement?' I asked the Chief Secretary.

It was, I saw at once, a stupid question. He was clearly put out. 'You made too much of it all,' he said. 'In your place I should have fined Hughes five rupees and left out all the lecture you gave him.'

'Fined him for boxing his servant's ears? But that would have reduced the case to an absurdity, while there was really something in it,' I urged.

Mr. Lloyd looked meaningly at Mr. Booth Gravely.

At this moment, Sir Charles was seen approaching. He shook hands with us and said to me:

'You must be feeling tired, and glad your case is over.'

Then he observed generally: 'What the Burmans objected to was the idea that we don't treat servants here in the same way as we do at home.'

Considering that Sir Charles had not handled the papers and was an extremely busy man it was remarkable how he penetrated straight to the point. I thought that Mr. Lloyd looked slightly discomposed. However, the subject was changed; Sir Charles gave a few parting instructions and entered his coach.

When the train had gone Swami Shayamananda, the head of a Hindu mission and hostel in the town, who had been within earshot, came up to me and said simply:

'The Governor is a gentleman.'

[1] Now Sir Idwal Lloyd.

I left the station feeling that I had by no means heard the last of the Hughes case. From the attitude of the two high officials I had spoken to on the platform it was clear that my judgement had offended some people. I believed that what I had said was true and proper to the occasion, and I had been simple enough to think that the ordinary man must agree with me. But I now began to see that I was mistaken.

That evening I went to the Pegu Club and sat down at one of the little tables in the bar. It was a Saturday, exactly a week since I had been there after the end of the murder trial, but there was a marked difference in the atmosphere. Several of the leading merchants were having drinks and they looked across at me with little friendliness. I observed Mr. McDonnell in conference with them. However, members of my own service came and spoke to me. From the moment I had entered there was only one topic of conversation. Each member was trying to get the rest to listen while he told them what he would have done had he been in my place. Some of my friends were defending my action. There was one little fellow, senior to me in the service, whose views were inclined to be old-fashioned and stiff, but he said to me: 'When I read your judgement for the first time I thought you were wrong to have blamed Hughes in any way, and then I remembered your phrase—"what was the value of sleeve-links beside a man's life?"—and I saw you were right.'

Others, however, did not take this human view. My judgement appeared to them damaging to white prestige; it sounded like an admission that the English attitude to the native inhabitants was something as it had been described by the inhabitants themselves.

'We ought to be very careful not to admit anything like that these days,' said a rice miller. 'I am not saying that everything Hughes did was wise, I can even see why it might have been worth his while to have been more liberal to the woman. But all that is beside the point. It was not necessary for Collis to draw attention to such short-comings. His criticisms are bound to involve us all in a general unpopularity at a time when it is essential we should preserve appearances.'

'I'm afraid I can't agree with that argument,' said a friend of mine. 'Collis's judgement can be taken as the English view. Supposing he had not said what he did the Burmese would have felt we were all against them. As things are, I wouldn't mind betting, if you keep your mouth shut, you'll be more popular with your workmen than you were before.'

'I daresay,' retorted the miller, 'but that means throwing over a white man.'

'You can't have it every way,' replied the other. 'You say it's bad for you to be embroiled with the Burmese, but you seem to be heading straight for it.'

'I'm not going to let down a white man,' said the miller sullenly.

'But that's exactly what you are doing, letting down all the white men.'

'I don't know what you mean. We must all stand together.'

'Against the Burmese?'

'You know quite well I don't mean that.'

I forget the miller's name; the other speaker was the Civilian, Philip Fogarty.

But it was evident that the miller's way of thinking held the floor. I reflected with uneasiness that if this was the majority view in the Pegu Club, which was chiefly official, the Gymkhana and Boat Clubs, both mercantile strong-holds, were sure to be solidly against me.

In the face of this opposition, I began to feel less sure of what I had done. Was I, perhaps, wrong? Had I been tactless, said too much, been too severe? Was Mr. McDon-nell right and should I have given Hughes no more than an indulgent rap over the knuckles and told him to study the Burmese temperament? It was hard to say. To judge an action one required the long view of time; to be sure whether a thing of that sort was well done was as difficult as to judge correctly about a contemporary work of art. When the action is your own, certainty in such a matter is perhaps impossible on the intellectual plane.

My confidence undermined by these reflections I could no longer bear the unpleasantness which surrounded me, and, saying good night to my friends, I went back to my house. Dinner did not restore my poise. When it was over I went into my study and looked through my Chinese collection. This contact with old works of art seemed to free me from my *malaise*. I began to see things more clearly. If I had said nothing there would have been no public statement of opinion about a matter which the whole country had been debating for over a month. My silence would have been taken to mean official condonation, and the Government in Burma and, for that matter, the whole English nation would have been saddled for ever with having condoned what they should not have condoned. More stupid still—they would have been represented as condoning what in their own practice they did not condone. The commotion was all nonsense. The English were very good to their servants as a rule. When one of their number fell short of the usual standard the community should be strong enough publicly to disapprove. This standing shoulder to shoulder was futile and undignified. It ran counter to what was best in our character. We occupied a great position in the East. It was impossible for us to be too fair, impossible to be too grand. It was not to our credit that there had been any fear in the Burmese mind that the trial would not be a fair one. It should have been assumed that in the natural course of things the District Magistrate would so conduct himself in his handling of the case that what he did and said would represent the true

English tradition. There had been no such assumption. I remembered the monks and the forbidding women. By God, I thought, I was right! What an appalling solecism it would have been had I failed to speak the English idiom. It was the English who were on trial, not Hughes at all. Millions were watching to see how we should behave in a situation which called for a little more than the usual detachment. I felt a profound gratitude that something had guided me to do what I now clearly saw to have been, beyond question, right.

On the Monday I was at work again as usual at court. I decided to bother no more about the late case. Feeling would subside, people would come to their right mind. The merchants, who had done their best to raise a doubt about their own essential good nature, would see daylight, if they were given time.

In this I was not mistaken. Ten days after the judgement there appeared in the *Rangoon Daily News*, a nationalist paper, a leading article which was a moderately worded plea for some compensation to Ma Kywé, the widow. Surprise was expressed that compensation had not already been paid. If Messrs. Hughes and Mitchell had no money, it was suggested that 'the great company which through two of its employees has become associated with the tragedy should in deference alone to public sentiment in the case of Ma Kywé deal generously with so pitiable a claimant upon its bounty'.

Whether influenced or not by this plea, the management of Steel Brothers did the generous thing and gave Ma Kywé the substantial sum of seventy-five pounds. Shortly afterwards they transferred Mr. Hughes to one of their branches in India.

CHAPTER FOUR

1. SEDITION

O n New Year's Day, while we were all wishing each other a happy new year, there came into my mind what had been foretold of 1930—the Burmese belief that it would see momentous events. The Hughes case had shaken me, and I hoped that if 1930 was to be an *annus mirabilis* I should have no more than the normal responsibility of my office. At the back of my mind was the monk's warning— 'a conflict with people of your own nation.' But perhaps the conflict was over with the Hughes trial. I sincerely hoped that this was so and that I should not be called upon to try any more cases where fundamental principles were involved.

If momentous events were likely there was the further likelihood that they would be connected with the nationalist movement in India. Burma was a part of the Indian Empire, and though the Burmese had little in common with the Indians they had the same aspiration for a free government, and found what was happening across the bay very relevant to their case. Lord Irwin[1] had been Viceroy for two and a half years. During that time Gandhi had been released from the prison in which Lord Reading had placed him, and though Lord Irwin had tried to satisfy him and his Congress by inducing the Secretary of State to send out the Commission under Sir John Simon before it was due the Congress was not satisfied, for they knew that the Commission would not recommend a free government.

[1]Now Lord Halifax.

81

At the beginning of 1930 Gandhi was organizing a great demonstration of mass disobedience, a method of putting pressure on the Government which he had tried before without much success, for it led to violence, and violence was bad tactics. He wanted his followers to appear lowly and oppressed; violence would alienate the sympathy which he courted. The demonstration of 1930 was to take the form of a breach of the salt laws. In India salt was a Government monopoly. No one was allowed to make salt unless he had a licence from the Excise Department and no individual licences were issued, except in certain specified areas where there were salt mines. Thus, even a village situated on the sea-shore or on a tidal creek was not per-mitted to condense sea water into brine by evaporation and boil it down to salt for its own consumption. This salt monopoly was defended as a way of taxing everybody, but it was unpopular, and Gandhi showed acumen in selecting it for his demonstration of non-violent civil disobedience. His intention was to walk from his Ashram, a monastic institution he had founded, to the sea coast with many followers and there openly make salt on the beach. He calculated that he and his followers would be imprisoned, as they would refuse to pay fines, and hoped that his example would be followed by thousands and tens of thousands, and that thereby he would be able to move, as it were, a gigantic vote of censure upon the Government, so intensely meant that multitudes would offer themselves for imprisonment, creating such a universal frown of disap-probation that the Government would no longer feel sure of its own virtue, and would falter and so grant the popu-lar demand for a free government. This original pro-gramme of constitutional agitation, both clever and mild, was profoundly suited to the Indian mind. It was as strange to the Burmese as to us.

During the first week of March 1930 Gandhi sent his famous ultimatum to Lord Irwin, whom in some sort he loved. 'Dear Friend,' he wrote, 'I must destroy your Government.'

To the English in Rangoon the spectacle was not that of two great men manoeuvring for a grapple. Mr. Churchill had still to call Gandhi the 'naked faquir', but it was in such guise that he appeared to most, an indecent figure capering insolently before the King-Emperor's vice-regent. As to the vice-regent, he was already called a traitor by some and it was darkly whispered that if he continued to traffic with the King's enemies he would come to an impeachment. That Gandhi was a world figure, whose life and thought had been studied by thousands in every country, was unintelligently denied. The millers, timber merchants, oil magnates, and mine managers, who congregated at seven o'clock in the clubs, did not seek to understand the drama which was being played out across the bay, but it alarmed and angered them as inconsistent with their conception of a commercial empire.

It was at this time of crisis, on 16 March, that the Commissioner of Police, Mr. Merrikin, came to see me. He was a small man with a dry manner. When he was seated opposite to me in my chamber above the court-room he opened some papers and said:

'Here is a warrant made out for Sen Gupta's arrest. The Governor-in-Council hopes you will sign it.'

Sen Gupta was Mayor of Calcutta and Gandhi's chief lieutenant in Bengal.

Merrikin proceeded: 'You remember those speeches which he made in Rangoon when he was here last month?'

'I remember seeing in the newspapers that he was here, but I don't remember that he made a speech.'

'He made three speeches and these are the transcripts of two of them,' said the Commissioner, handing me a batch of papers. 'They are seditious,' he went on, 'and if you will read those portions which I have marked in blue pencil I think you will agree with me.'

I looked through the marked passages. In one of them I noticed that Sen Gupta had used some hard expressions about Sir Charles Innes.

'Has the Government Advocate's opinion been taken?' I asked.

'Yes, the Government Advocate has advised that a *prima facie* case of sedition lies.'

'It seems rather an extreme course to arrest the Mayor of Calcutta and bring him down here, unless the speeches were very bad,' I said. 'At a casual glance I see nothing much.'

'The Law Officers were satisfied a case lay.'

'There is a case, certainly,' I admitted, 'but is it of sufficient weight?'

'We have considered that,' replied the Commissioner. 'The Governor-in-Council wishes to take action.'

It was clear that I was asked to sign the warrant as a routine act, and it was my duty to sign it, on being satisfied that the usual formalities had been carried out. My opinion was not sought either on the legal or on the executive aspects. Nor would it have been usual for the Government to seek it, for I was not a legal expert, and Mr. Merrikin, not I, was responsible for the administration of law and order. Accordingly I signed without further parley and Mr. Merrikin took his departure.

When he had gone I remained in thought for some time. I knew that if Sen Gupta were brought to Rangoon I should have to try him, because the offence with which he was to be charged had taken place within my jurisdiction. The trial was bound to be very sensational. It was unusual for one provincial government to arrest a prominent public man residing under another provincial government on a charge of sedition committed within the area of the first. The excitement in Bengal would be intense, for Sen Gupta was probably among the five best-known men in India at the time. Educated at Cambridge and called to the Bar, he

had made a lucrative practice for himself in Calcutta.
After the war he had gone into politics and on the death of
the great nationalist, C. R. Das, had become the leader of
the Congress Party in his province. His followers called him
the 'Lion of Bengal'. His wife was an Englishwoman.

This was the celebrity whom Sir Charles had decided to
arrest and whom I should have to try. I realized at once
that I should be thrust into the public eye. The Burma
Government, it was true, frequently instituted prosecutions
for sedition committed within the province and took its
chance of getting a conviction, but the prosecution of a Sen
Gupta was very different to an ordinary provincial prosecution. The news of his arrest would be news all the world
over; it would appear at once in the London papers; the
Indian Press would declare it proof, if proof were needed,
of the heavy hand of the authorities. In such circumstances
it was highly desirable that the arrest should be justified by
a conviction. If the case went wrong and I was unable to
convict I should be delivering the Government to wide
public criticism. With a cold feeling I remembered that on
a first glance the case had not seemed to me too strong.
Coming so soon after the Hughes case I was not sure
Whether my nerves would stand the strain of such a State
trial. But there was clearly no way out of it. I should have
to take the case.

Wishing to refresh my memory of the law I opened the
annotated edition of the Penal Code on my table and
turned up section 124A, in which sedition is defined. I had
always admired the rhythmical flow of the words; as a
piece of legal English it was admirable. Tradition says it
was drafted by Macaulay. 'Whoever by words, either
spoken or written, or by signs, or by visible representation,
or otherwise brings or attempts to bring into hatred or
contempt, or excites or attempts to excite disaffection
towards His Majesty or the Government established by law
in British India, shall be punished,' etc. The penalty could

extend to a long term of imprisonment with hard labour, a sentence of from two to five years being quite usual.

As one looked at it, it was a formidable section. By a wink which attempted to bring the Government into contempt with those who saw the wink you might be committing sedition. If at the mention of His Majesty you shrugged your shoulders, your intention being to excite your companions to disaffection towards him, you could be convicted.

I turned up the rulings by the various High Courts and perceived that the section had never been used in such fashion. Its main object was to forestall a breach of the peace. It envisaged the poor and the ignorant prompted to violence by unscrupulous harangue. But though the government which had made it the law of India had in the forefront of their mind rebellions caused by criminal agitation, they had drafted it to cover any eventuality. A man was guilty if he tried to excite hatred against the Government, even if he failed to do so; nor was he innocent if in exciting hatred he had spoken against violence. It was enough if he meant his audience to feel contempt, and it was beside the point whether they felt it or not. Thus, a speech which imputed dishonesty to the Government might be seditious, and a speech which made use of such an imputation to advocate quite a legitimate policy might equally be seditious.

In short the law was so wide that it left a great discretion to the executive. Under it they had the power to prosecute their political opponents, and in 1930, when the whole of India was ringing with speeches advocating the introduction of a new and reformed government, that was a useful power. Many of these speeches were seditious within the meaning of Section 124A, for though they advocated nothing worse than a change in the constitution they made their points by abusing the existing government. They had, moreover, been highly successful, because by then the diarchical Government was held in hatred and contempt by large numbers of persons. So well was all this understood that Pandit Malaviya about this date was able to say in the Legislative Assembly in Delhi: 'It is the duty of every Indian that he should bring into hatred and preach hatred against the existing form of government.' At which remark the President thought it unnecessary to do more than call out 'Order! Order!'

The fact was that no-one was prosecuted unless he sought to induce in his hearers an instant and dangerous hatred. What might amount to a dangerous hatred had to be determined in each case. So when a man was prosecuted under Section 124A it was generally a very bad case and he received a heavy sentence. The police did not advise a prosecution where the sedition was technical or mild, for if magistrates were to impose correspondingly technical or mild sentences the crime of sedition would lose its dark repute and ignorant people think that disaffection towards His Majesty was grown no worse than petty assault or drunkenness.

Technically the fellow who said, 'You should condemn the men who have robbed you of your country as you do the common thief who takes your purse,' uttered a seditious sentence, but in practice the police ignored such remarks, until like the word diarchy itself they came to be regarded as no more than abuse.

As I searched the code, with its commentaries, such was the law and usage which I found, and had I not already come tentatively to a contrary opinion I should have supposed that when Sen Gupta was in Rangoon he had attempted to excite hatred and contempt towards the Burma Government of so dangerous a type that it was essential to lock him up, even though he had left the country and was resident in Calcutta, which is as far from Rangoon as Rome is from London.

2. THE ARREST OF THE MAYOR

The warrant of arrest was entrusted to two Burmese
police officers, who set out for Calcutta at once by steamer.
They arrived there early on the morning of 13 March and
reported themselves to the Commissioner of Police. That
officer was expecting them: the Government of Burma had
not made its plunge without informing the Indian authorities what it was doing. The Burma police officers were
accordingly shown in without delay, and when they had
produced their credentials the Assistant Commissioner of
the south district of the city was deputed to conduct them
to Sen Gupta's residence.

Sen Gupta did not know that what he had said in Rangoon a month before had seriously offended the Burma
Government. For some time before his visit he had been
feeling unwell, and early in 1930 his doctor, diagnosing
abnormally high blood-pressure, had advised him to take
a sea voyage for the sake of his health. On 1 February he
had left Calcutta with his wife, intending to make the
round trip to Singapore and back. He arrived at Rangoon
on 3 February, but did not land. A Mr. Abdul Bari
Chowdhury, the managing director of the Bengal-Burma
Steam Navigation Company, called on him on board, and,
before leaving, expressed the hope that on his return from
Singapore he would come ashore, when they would all be
very pleased to see him. If he could put in a word against
the proposed separation of Burma from India it would be
a help, particularly to the Bengal-Burma Steam Navigation Company, which, as an Indian concern, might suffer
should Burma and India be politically severed.

Sen Gupta had then gone on to Singapore, and on the
18th of February his ship touched at Rangoon again. He
was induced to land this time and stay over till the next

boat. An address of welcome was prepared by a number of leading men, including Captain Rushall, the Mayor of Rangoon, who signed in his private capacity as a citizen, and it was presented to Mr. Sen Gupta at 5 p.m. at a meeting in Fytche Square. Mr. Paw Tun, the barrister, was in the chair. The usual polite introductory speeches were made, Sen Gupta being saluted as a great political leader, the head of the Bengal Congress and Mahatma Gandhi's lieutenant. The citizens who had arranged the meeting were chiefly those who were opposed to the separation of Burma from India, that is to say firstly the Indians resident in Rangoon, who not unnaturally preferred a constitution wherein Burma would be under the orders of an Indian government, and secondly those few Burmans who feared that if Burma were separated the local government's advice to the Simon Commission would be taken and she would be given an inferior constitution. They all wanted to take advantage of the presence of so influential a political leader as Sen Gupta, and to get him to warn the Burmese of the danger they ran by cutting themselves off from the great Indian paladins, who were strong enough to stand up to the British.

Sen Gupta, who was feeling the better for his sea voyage, though his blood-pressure was still too high, rose to respond to the valedictory address. He had not prepared a speech, but he was an accomplished orator and had no difficulty in improvising. Moreover, the subject was familiar to him. From his point of view it was lunacy on the part of the Burmans to think of standing alone at that juncture. Gandhi, the greatest man in the East, was about to launch his non-violent War of Independence. They were on the eve of a long wrangle with the British. The Simon Commission Report was due in four months. It would recommend what India could not accept and it would also recommend separation for Burma. The Indian tussle would go on, but if Burma accepted separation she would be out of it. In the end India would secure better terms and Burma would not be able to share in them. When India eventually was enjoying a free government Burma would find that she had been tricked by the bait of separation into a constitution far less independent. To Sen Gupta it seemed extraordinary that the Burmese did not see this. Like all Indians he had a poor opinion of their brains. He was certain that the British Government would cheat them if it possibly could. It did not strike him as sense that the British would be obliged to give Burma the same concessions as they gave to India. Fair play would demand it, but he did not believe that they were actuated by fair play. His experience as a politician had made him despair of their character. Though his wife was English and he liked English games and clothes and food and at one time had had many English friends, the bitterness of the political battle had soured him against them. It was all a huge racket. Had not Sir Charles Innes declared for separation and at the same time advised Sir John Simon that the Burmese were only fit as yet for a limited form of self-government? If the Burmese were fools enough to take the bait, they were done for, and they would deserve the humiliation which was being prepared for them.

In that sense Sen Gupta addressed the audience in Fytche Square under the shadow of the Soolay Pagoda. He spoke in English, because he did not know Burmese and thought it inadvisable to use Hindustani. But the crowd was almost entirely composed of Indians. Most of those present, therefore, did not understand what he said, but as his speech would afterwards be circulated in the Burmese Press, the promoters were satisfied that it would have its effect.

Two days later, under the same auspices, he addressed an audience in one of the public halls. The subject was the same—an Indo-Burman entente. There were a number of Burmese students present on this occasion, not much more forward in English than the crowd in the square. He solemnly warned them not to trust the British if they wanted a free constitution; the Indians were the people to trust; they must all stand together.

On 21 February, the next day, he made his last speech. It was in Fytche Square again. Mr. Abdul Bari Chowdhury was in the chair, still thinking about his steamers and how awkward it would be if, as a result of separation, there was no annual flow of labourers for them to carry from India to Burma. Mr. Paw Tun sat on the platform with other reputable citizens. The audience was not more Burmese than before, the truth being that the Burmese did not flock to hear Indian politicians, no matter how distinguished.

Somewhat neglected in this way by the persons he had come to help, Sen Gupta got on to his feet for the third time and for the third time, in English, begged the Burmans not to be fools. They could depend on a fair deal from India in the hour of victory, but if they cut themselves off from that source of power and put their trust in the British, they would get the reward they deserved for being so credulous—the constitution Sir Charles Innes had in mind for them.

The people on the platform were not English and so had no objection to hearing the English abused, but they listened calmly to what was said because it was so familiar and because they knew a great deal more about Burma, and what was practicable in Burma, than did the speaker. As for the ragged and dirty crowd of Indians who composed the bulk of the audience, they had no idea what Sen Gupta was talking about, but they knew he was a big gentleman from Calcutta and they had all come to have a look at his face.

On each occasion reporters were present and a summary of the speeches appeared in the next morning's newspapers. The C.I.D. detectives were also busy and brought their chief a word for word transcript.

In a broad way this was what had happened in Rangoon

in February; and when Sen Gupta heard, nearly a month later, that a couple of Burma policemen were waiting on his steps to serve a warrant on him, he was astounded. ' Can it be those speeches?' he is reported to have said.

The policemen were shown in and served the warrant. Sen Gupta read it through—it *was* the speeches. He found himself charged with sedition and was to appear before the courts in Rangoon on 18 March.

'I am instructed to offer you bail in two sureties of five thousand rupees each,' announced the Assistant Commissioner who accompanied the Burma policemen.

'I refuse to furnish bail,' replied Sen Gupta at once.

By the rules of Congress its members neither furnished bail, pleaded, nor paid fines in political cases.

The Government of Bengal had anticipated such a move and the Assistant Commissioner had his instructions. To take the Mayor of Calcutta in custody through his own streets and incarcerate him in the city lock-up, and that on the behest of the Burma Government, one of the junior governments in India, was not to the taste of the Bengal authorities. Such a course would probably throw the whole city into tumult. So it had been arranged that, if Sen Gupta refused bail, he was to be detained that night in his house. Next morning he would be put on board the mail-boat and taken to Rangoon.

The Assistant Commissioner carried out his orders, posted policemen, and left the premises.

News of the mayor's arrest was carried by reporters immediately to the offices of the nationalist Press and within an hour extra editions of the evening newspapers were being sold. It was still early in the afternoon. As soon as the shopkeepers realized what had happened they put up their shutters; rickshaws ceased to ply; a *hartal* or day of mourning was spontaneously declared.

When the members of the corporation received the news they met and proceeded in a body to Sen Gupta's house, where certain other nationalist leaders were already assembled.

'What exactly did you say in Rangoon to set the Government of Burma on the war-path?' they asked.

'I can't remember exactly what I said,' replied the mayor. 'I spoke extempore on all three occasions. But the gist was that if the Burmans separated from us they would have to fight for freedom alone and in that case would certainly be defeated.'

'It's an awkward moment for you to get involved,' they said, 'with the Mahatma's march starting in a few weeks. Why did you bother about the Burmese?'

'It was the Indian community in Burma who asked me to speak.'

His friends then inquired whether he thought a conviction was possible.

'I am bound to be convicted,' he replied. 'You don't think they are going to haul me all the way to Rangoon and then acquit me! The Government of Burma isn't quite as stupid as that. It's all been fixed up.'

'You mean, it has been fixed with the Government of India?'

'Of course it has been fixed. I am to be the first casualty in Gandhi's campaign. They want me out of the way before the campaign starts. This is a trumped-up case.'

'But the magistrate can't go against the law.'

'It won't be necessary for him to do that. Any political speech which departs from generalities can be brought under the section. The magistrate will have no difficulty about the law. And he will not have all the facts before him. They will just prove the speeches and ask him to convict. As I do not intend to plead there will be no explanation of the circumstances. All will be over in a morning, and I shall probably get two years.'

His friends were depressed.

'But', he went on, 'there is no need to be upset. All this

falls out very well. Our policy is to invite unjust punishment; the masses must be roused. My conviction in Rangoon will be such an outrageous injustice that it will do the cause more good than anything I could have invented myself.'

They looked at him with sad admiration.

'But need you suffer quite so much?' inquired one of them. 'Imprisonment in Burma, far away from your family, and for a long term, will your health stand it? You have done enough already.'

'They are taking me there, anyhow. I must make the most of it.'

'And we shall do our best at this end,' they said, and returned home through the mourning streets.

At dawn the next day a large crowd gathered outside the mayor's house. With flowers in their hands the chief people came to the door, where Sen Gupta received them. Some offered him bunches or hung garlands round his neck, while others painted his forehead with vermilion, for the day was the festival of Holi, when it was customary to redden the forehead.

In due course the police escort arrived in a car. The S.S. *Sirdhana* was scheduled to leave Outram Ghat at nine o'clock. Sen Gupta entered the car and was driven through the crowd. Some of the people were weeping and some shouted 'long live the revolution'. At the ghat an enormous concourse was waiting.

The escort quickly took him on board the mail-boat. Leaning from the rail, he saluted the people. The excitement increased. A band of volunteers climbed on board and attempted to hoist the tricolour national flag, but this was prevented. The siren went and he bade his family good-bye. To the leaders his last words were: 'You must stand by Mahatma Gandhi.'

The gangways were down and the ship began to move. A kind of frenzy seemed to shake the crowd as they saw their leader being taken from them. A cry went out: 'Down with the Union Jack.' Sen Gupta was still at the rail, waving his hand. The shouts were kept up till he passed out of sight.

As soon as he thought it politic to do so, he left the rail and went to his cabin, where he got rid of the flowers, washed the vermilion off his face, and changed out of his Indian clothes into a lounge suit. Then descending to the dining-saloon, he ordered breakfast. There was nothing sentimental about Sen Gupta. A realist, he knew that a lounge suit was the right dress in the first class of an English ship, just as the national costume with garlands was right for a crowd of Bengali supporters. And he was decidedly hungry after the excitements of the morning; and he liked a dish of eggs and bacon.

3. THE MAYOR ARRIVES

While these events were happening across the bay, events which were reported by telegram from Calcutta in the Rangoon papers, I had received from the police the record of the case, that is to say, all the relevant papers supported by the exhibits, which were the transcripts of the speeches made on 20 and 21 February. I noticed that no witnesses were being called, except formal evidence that the speeches had been delivered.

I sat down now to study the speeches. Were they, as I had supposed at first sight, more technically than actually seditious? I found it exceedingly difficult to make up my mind. As a rule, of course, a magistrate does not try to come to any sort of conclusion about a case until he has heard the evidence. But the present trial was rather different.

All the evidence was already on the record, as the prosecution was calling no witnesses; the charge of sedition was founded on the written evidence of two of the three speeches.

Repeated perusal of the speeches made me feel that I must have more light if I were to decide fairly on the degree in which they were seditious. I must have in evidence as complete a picture as possible of Sen Gupta's visit to Rangoon. The first speech, for instance, should be produced. It was on record that U Paw Tun, Abdul Bari Chowdhury, and other well-known people had promoted the speeches and had heard them delivered. To have the testimony of such people surely was essential? When the time came I should have to call some of them, whether the prosecution liked it or not.

The more I thought of what loomed ahead of me, the less pleasant grew the prospect. Sometimes the case appeared so weak that I became doubtful even about a technical conviction. But I did not see what I could do. It was no good my going to the Governor and telling him I thought the case weak. He had the opinion of the Law Officers and would certainly not consider mine a better opinion. Moreover, as the trying magistrate, it would be very improper for me to express any opinion at that stage. My opinion was not required until the Government Advocate should place the facts and the law before me. In any event, Sir Charles could not withdraw. Sen Gupta had been arrested; he was on the sea and was due in Rangoon at 7 a.m. on 17 March. To suppose that on landing he could be informed that the case had been withdrawn was to suppose an impossibility.

There was no-one in authority whom I could consult, no one from whom I could obtain advice. The Law Officers, some judge of the High Court, a lawyer—I passed them all in review. Insuperable difficulties existed about going to any of them. I saw that I must rely entirely upon my own judgement.

In the course of the week-end, the 15–16 March, I ran into Frank Fearnley-Whittingstall, who was Deputy Commissioner of Police under Mr. Menikin.

'Well,' he said, 'how do you feel? It's going to be a lively case.'

'In what way, specially?'

'There'll be an enormous crowd and possibly a free fight. We're taking elaborate police precautions.'

'Tell me,' I said. 'Why did H.E. launch this prosecution? What's the real truth?'

'He didn't want Indian agitators poking their noses into Burma.'

'Sen Gupta was maddening enough, of course—coming over here to upset the separation plan.'

"Not only that, H.E. wants to keep Burma out of the Indian mix-up. When the C.I.D. drew his attention to the speeches, it seemed a wonderful opportunity to discourage fellows like Sen Gupta from putting ideas into Burmans' heads.'

'What about the reference to himself in the speeches?'

'I shouldn't think he bothered. He's above that sort of thing, though of course everyone will say he sanctioned the prosecution for that reason.'

'But do you personally think Sen Gupta could influence the Burmans?'

Frank smiled. 'Sen Gupta knows nothing whatever about Burma. The Burmese have got their own ideas and are not going to take advice from him. There are things happening now in the villages of which none of us has the slightest idea.'

I remembered this remark ten months later when we heard that the strange being called Saya San had been crowned King of Burma. At the very moment we were speaking he was touring the villages and whispering into the ears of farmers and their men privy conspiracy and rebellion, beside which Sen Gupta's tourist stuff in Fytche Square was utterly insignificant.

On Monday, 17 March, I was up early. The arrangements
were that Mr. Phipps, Superintendent of the River Police,
should meet the mail-boat when she berthed about seven
o'clock and bring Sen Gupta straight to my house, where
Mr. Merrikin and myself would be waiting.

When Mr. Phipps arrived at Brooking Street wharf he
found a small crowd of Bengalis by the waterside. They
were dressed in white homespun cotton clothes with shawls,
and white caps, rather like military forage caps in shape,
were on their heads. From time to time one of their number,
an elderly man with a white moustache, blew wailing blasts
on a conch shell. The melancholy sound was carried by the
north wind over the river crowded with shipping, through
which the mail-boat *Sirdhana* was threading her way.

Mr. Phipps was congratulating himself on his luck that
so few sympathizers had come to meet Sen Gupta when
news was brought that outside one of the dock gates were
three motor-buses, one of which was full of monks, the
other two containing the formidable-looking Burmese
women who wore homespun clothes. The object of these
people, presumably, was to follow the police car carrying
Sen Gupta, and to make, as they drove, some kind of
demonstration.

These monks and women were the same people who had
crowded into my court during the Hughes case. As old-
fashioned nationalists, who understood nothing of
Gandhi's non-violent philosophy, and who, indeed, had
no feeling but contempt for Indians, it was strange that
they should meet Sen Gupta on the wharf. But there was
an explanation. They had already heard of Saya San and
his aims, were already secretly plotting rebellion by force
and magic. In their eyes the Bengali leader stood for
revolution. They neither knew nor cared that it was a constitutional revolution. That he was a revolutionary was
good enough, and that he had abused the Governor en-
deared him to them still more.

When Mr. Phipps heard of their sinister arrival he gave orders that Sen Gupta's car should be driven out of the docks by a different gate. In that way he hoped to shake them off. He did not fancy the idea of a procession through the town with the women yelling at him, nor did he care to think of arriving at my house in such company.

The S.S. *Sirdhana* came alongside and he went on board. Sen Gupta was ready in the saloon; he had changed back into his nationalist clothes, and, like his compatriots on the wharf, was wrapped in a shawl of homespun and wore a white cap. Mr. Phipps took charge of him at once and escorted him quickly towards the waiting car, but the men on the wharf recognized the tall figure of the Indian patriot. A blast was sounded on the conch; cries of *Bande Mataram* (Hail to the Mother) were raised and they surrounded the car. Sen Gupta was then garlanded with roses.

Mr. Phipps warned the crowd to stand back and the car started. The gate where the buses were waiting was avoided and a dash was made for the west gate farther along. The women in the buses saw what was happening and told their drivers to hurry, but before they could reach the other gate the police car shot out and was lost to sight.

Using strong language the women shouted at their drivers to follow. They careered round the town at a rattling pace, visiting the jail, the lock-up, and finally Fytche Square, where a few Indians were waiting expectantly, but there was no sign and no news of Sen Gupta. That he had been driven straight to my house occurred to nobody. The women by now were infuriated. They had been up since five o'clock, without even a cup of tea. 'What d'you take us for!' they asked the monks. 'Drive us home, you bastards!' they told the drivers. In extreme dudgeon they went off lavishing epithets upon Mr. Phipps which proved them to be persons of the richest imagination.

Meanwhile the police car sped by devious ways to my gate. Apparently Sen Gupta had got rid of the garland, for when he alighted at my porch he was wearing no roses. Mr. Merrikin had already arrived, and we received him in the hall. His manner was distant. He was a stout man, over six feet high, with a humorous expression; his shawl, which was like a toga, gave him an air of the forum. I took him into my study. It was still very early, hardly seven-thirty, and the sun was slanting into the garden, a strong light entering the room, which caused the greens and reds of my porcelain to smoulder. I asked him to sit down and offered him a cup of tea. He said he had had his tea, but he regarded me with rather more interest.

'I understand', I went on, 'that you have been ill and are still not strong.'

'My blood-pressure remains rather high,' he replied, 'but this second voyage, which in the ordinary way I could not have afforded myself, has done me good.'

I did not smile.

'Your trial', I explained, 'is fixed for to-morrow at 11 a.m. I have obtained the sanction of the High Court, and if you like you can have bail. The amount they fixed is nominal.'

'I'm afraid I can't avail myself of bail. To do so would be to recognize your court and, if I may say so without appearing, rude, that is impossible.'

This remark galled me. To be told bluntly that the English courts, renowned in the world for fairness, had some opposite reputation in India hit me in a soft place. I determined to force him, before I had done, to admit that my court at least was as fair as any court could be.

Disguising my feelings, I said: 'I anticipated your difficulty in the matter of bail. When one is not very well Congress rules must be tiresome. Would you like to stay in a private house by the lakes? Perhaps I could arrange that for you.'

'Thank you,' he said, 'but wouldn't that mean bail?'

'Oh, not at all!' I protested. 'Bail?—Oh, no—there'd be a guard, a strict guard.'

'Well,' he said, 'that's kind. I'd like that.' His expression had changed slightly.

At the moment Mr. Merrikin was speaking to Mr. Phipps at the hall door. I went out of the room and made the suggestion to him. 'This bail business is only a game to put us in the wrong. It's sounder tactics to treat him to a house. They let him stay in his house in Calcutta.'

'I can't accept the responsibility,' said the Commissioner.

'It would calm the public, you know, and save you trouble in the long run. After all, if he gave bail we should have less control over what he might do.'

'I can't accept the responsibility,' repeated Mr. Merrikin, 'and I don't see why I should if he refuses bail.'

I returned to my study and told Sen Gupta that I could not arrange it; he would have to be lodged in the prison. 'And there is one thing more,' I added. 'About your defence—are you engaging counsel? If so, an adjournment may be necessary.'

'I am precluded from making a defence.'

There was nothing more to be said and the police took him away to the jail.

4. THE TRIAL OPENS

When I approached my court the next morning I found the street almost blocked with Indians of the lower class. A strong force of Burman police was on duty under a Mr. Sadiq Ali, who by a coincidence was a Bengali, the only Bengali officer in the force. The English sergeants of the

Mogul Guard were there, too, under Inspector Crisp, and I was informed that mounted police were standing by off-scene. Trouble was clearly expected, as Whittingstall had said. There were no Burmans about, however, no sign of the monks and the hard-faced women. Perhaps they felt that they had been made fools of for an Indian. Certainly none of them appeared during any part of the trial.

As I entered by the side door I could hear a hum of voices from the court-room. It was evidently packed with spectators. I went upstairs to my chamber, and pending Sen Gupta's arrival passed short orders on the petitions of the day.

At 11.25 I heard loud shouts from the crowd, and looking out of my window, which commanded the street in the direction of the prison, saw an open car approaching in which was seated Sen Gupta beside Mr. Hall of the Imperial Police. He was receiving a great ovation from the crowd, to which he replied good-humouredly by waving his hand. Cries of 'Bande Mataram' and 'Victory to Gupta' rose on all sides. The Mogul Guard loosened their truncheons and opened a passage to the door of the court-room, into which Sen Gupta was hurried as well as could be. The door was banged after him and the crowd bellowed dismally its despair. Evidently the Sen Gupta case was going to be sensational from every point of view. I wondered vaguely whether the crowd, which numbered over a thousand, would break into the court-room and rescue their hero, and, if so, whether the rule about a captain on a bridge applied by analogy to a magistrate on a bench. Should I have to go down with the bench? But I had no time to brood on this problem; indeed, I was so taken up with the legal task before me that I ceased to bother about the shouts from the street, nor did I inquire whether the guards were adequate. My clerks were Burmese and seemed calm and cheerful. Having little opinion of Indians they felt no alarm; it was a gala day for them, one of the great days of their lives.

When I was told that Sen Gupta was in his place and all was ready I descended the stairs. At the door of the court my old *chaprassie* called out, and, as everybody stood up, I mounted the bench, from which I bowed to the Government Advocate, Mr. Eggar. The court was crowded to its utmost capacity with Indians of the upper class. The whole Indian Bar was present in a body and I noticed Mr. Tyabji, the leader of the Congress Party in Burma. The presence of these gentlemen was reassuring, for all their inclination would be to keep the enthusiasm of the mob within bounds. In any assault upon the court-room they themselves would be the first target, as they were jammed under the bench, while I had a convenient exit behind it. Sen Gupta had a chair next a friend of his, a Mr. Sen, one of the Calcutta legal family of that name. Someone had given him a newspaper, but he laid it down and rose to his feet with the rest when I came in, thereby, I was afterwards informed, neglecting to comply with the rules of Congress and to that minimum extent recognizing the court before which he stood arraigned. I was glad to note his diminished rigour and to observe that, though he immediately took up his newspaper again and began to study the latest tele-grams about Gandhi and the campaign to break the salt laws, his expression was not severe, and when he whis-pered to Mr. Sen his face was animated.

'May it please your Worship.' It was the Government Advocate opening his case. Mr. Eggar was a tall man with an eccentric humour. No-one in Rangoon had a better heart.

'Your Worship has the text of the speeches before you and I am only tendering formal evidence,' he said, putting Mr. Merrikin in the box.

That little man had a dogged brave air and he described how he had been instructed to bring the prosecution. 'The

speeches of the 20th and 21st of September were taken
down in shorthand by Mr. Dancing of the C.I.D., who
attended the meetings,' he explained.

When the Government Advocate had done with him, by
normal procedure he should have been cross-examined by
counsel for the defence or by the accused himself, if not
represented. Accordingly I turned to Mr. Sen Gupta, and
though I had every reason to know that he would decline
to cross-examine, as he had already intimated his detachment from the whole trial, I asked him whether he had any
questions to put to the Commissioner of Police before he
stepped down. To this Mr. Sen Gupta replied: 'I hope you
will not think me rude, but I do not propose to take any
voluntary part in these proceedings.'

Apparently this was a very polite speech for a member
of Congress to make to a magistrate who was trying him,
and the public in court looked at me with increased respect.

Mr. Dancing was the next witness. It was not very easy
to get him into the court, because of the pressure of the
crowd on both sides of the door. When the door was
opened two or three of the crowd were squeezed in along
with him and it was impossible to eject them. The noise
outside had sometimes been deafening and always been
inconvenient, but Mr. Merrikin, who, of course, was in
charge of the police arrangements, had not sent for rein-
forcements and cleared the street. He let the Indians shout
and sing because he thought noise was preferable to a
fight and he did not believe that, if they were allowed to
shout, they would resort to violence.

Mr. Dancing kissed the book and gave evidence in a
manner even more formal than his chief's. He had attended
the meetings and taken down the speeches. In answer to a
question by me he named the leading citizens who had been
present on each occasion, and those who had presided or
who themselves had made speeches.

When he left the box the Government Advocate said

that his case was complete. The transcripts of the speeches had not been challenged, the two formal witnesses he had called had not been cross-examined. It remained for him only to address me on the law.

I replied: 'Mr. Eggar, on an occasion of this kind where the accused person is a well-known figure and where public interest has been so marked that at times we have found it difficult to hear ourselves speak, it seems to me highly expedient to avoid any appearance of haste. In the ordinary way we could look to the accused to give us his explanation of the facts against him, but here we cannot do so, and I conceive it, therefore, to be my duty to ask for certain further particulars.'

I was determined to prevent the case being closed at that point, when a quantity of relevant evidence would be shut out which should be on the record if the trial were not to be a farce. I already knew that it was Sen Gupta's intention to turn it into a farce, to tempt me to hasten him wrong-fully to prison, and to tell the world that he had been unjustly sentenced. But I was not content to be used by him. The desire of Congress for a free government was as laudable as any other desire of the kind, but I was not going to help them to realize it by condemning Sen Gupta on formal evidence. That would be a piece of obscurantism from which my mind revolted. I saw and enjoyed the comedy but I was not willing to be the subject of it; to be a magistrate who, thinking to please a government, gave a wrongful order which also pleased its opponents; to be at once unfair and a fool.

When I said to Mr. Eggar that it was my duty to obtain further particulars he appeared very surprised. The Indian barristers below me began to whisper and Mr. Sen Gupta put down his newspaper.

Mr. Eggar rose. 'To what particulars does your Worship refer? A *prima facie* has been made out and your Worship is fully entitled to frame a charge.'

'To put it bluntly,' I replied, 'I want to hear what happened from first to last; I want it on record why Mr. Sen Gupta came to Burma; I want to examine the people who received him, and who also made speeches; and I want to know what their reactions were while he was speaking.'

Mr. Eggar consulted for a moment with his junior. 'If your Worship insists, the information can quickly be supplied,' he said. 'Some of the persons who were present when the speeches were delivered are in court to-day. I see Mr. Tyabji, for instance.'

I gave him a list of those I wanted to examine.

'All the gentlemen named can be produced within the space of an hour,' said he.

During these exchanges Mr. Sen Gupta forgot that it was his part to ignore the court and became extremely interested, while his barrister friends looked at me as if they saw a ghost.

I was about to ask Mr. Eggar to procure the attendance of the further witnesses when the crowd outside, as if scenting that something unusual was happening, made a rush at the door and were restrained with difficulty by the police. Shouting again was very loud and the whole street became a scene of disorder.

The Government Advocate: 'In view of the uproar I suggest that summonses be issued in the ordinary way and the witnesses be subpoenaed for to-morrow. Their attendance now can hardly be procured without much difficulty.'

'I have no objection, Mr. Eggar.'

Accordingly I adjourned the case till the next morning and the court rose. At that moment Mr. Sen asked whether Sen Gupta might have some lunch, either in the courtroom or in the car, before returning to the jail. I found the question somewhat irritating in that it was designed, I supposed, to maintain the fiction—for the reality had begun to disintegrate—that Sen Gupta was being badly treated.

'Mr. Sen Gupta can have his lunch just exactly wherever he likes,' I said, and left the bench.

When the crowd learned that the trial was over for the day it did not disperse at once, but waited until Sen Gupta had finished his lunch. Then it gave him an ovation as he left for the jail. I remained in my chamber for some hours attending to other business. At tea-time, when I drove home, the street was empty.

5. THE RIOT

On arrival next day at court I thought the crowd was thicker. Evidently Mr. Merrikin was of the same opinion, for he had posted more police. The sergeants of the Mogul Guard were in force. I noticed the very English countenances of Triggs and Tingley; and there was Sergeant Ryan, from over the Irish Sea, and Crown Sergeant Preston. Inspector Crisp saluted me smartly as I turned in.

Not a Burman was to be seen; the crowd was again wholly Indian, roughs and unemployed of the lowest class, but with a sprinkling of clerks and petty traders. It was hard to be sure who had brought them there, but presumably the hint had been given that a demonstration was necessary. I did not think that the Indian barristers had had anything to do with it, but that Mr. Tyabji must have given the hint.

Mr. Tyabji, who was an elected member of the legislature, was a very small man from Gujerat with a perky manner and a bright smile. When the present Duke of Windsor, then Prince of Wales, visited Burma Mr. Tyabji entertained some idea of a counter demonstration to draw attention to India's political needs. No government wants a royal personage to see more than it has been arranged for him to see, and Mr. Tyabji was arrested and sent to a remote country town called Papun, where he remained a fortnight and from which he returned with increased prestige.

As I recalled these facts I now became quite sure that the crowd hallooing at my windows had been sent for by Mr. Tyabji. The slight apprehension I had entertained the day before of an assault upon the court left my mind. The crowd was there to cheer and boo. It was quite harmless — that is to say as harmless as is any crowd while in a good humour. I hoped the police would keep it in a good humour.

As on previous occasions I went up to my chamber above the bench-room to transact current business before the case began. Barristers, police-officers, and pressmen were arriving in their cars, and the crowd cheered all of them heartily, regardless of colour or political complexion. From my window I could see men standing on the wall surrounding the compound of the Roman Catholic Church, a wall which was being repaired. Piles of bricks lay behind it.

At 11.20 a greater burst of cheering heralded the arrival of the prisoner, who as before sat back in the seat of an open car with Mr. Hall and acknowledged the acclamations with professional ease.

At 11.30 I came downstairs and took my seat on the bench.'

'Are the witnesses called by the court present?' I asked the Government Advocate.

Mr. Eggar had had the night to think over his position. That I had taken the conduct of the case out of his hands by exercising my statutory right of calling evidence had unsettled him. He could not object, because at law I was entitled to call evidence at any stage, if not satisfied that the whole truth was being given before me. But he did not

I continued to the best of my ability amid the uproar
ashes to examine Mr. Paw Tun, who stood like a rock
he witness box, answering my questions with perfe
cidity. After I had dismissed him I examined in succes-
on Captain Rushall, the Mayor of Rangoon, a true Con-
d figure; Abdul Bari Chowdhury, the manager of the
ngal-Burma Steam Navigation Company; Mr. Pillai,
ho represented West Rangoon Indian Constituency; and
number of others. Their evidence, which became easier
hear as the noise of the riot died away in the distance,
ovided me with the complete picture of Mr. Sen Gupta's
sit, and proved that his speeches had been delivered by
vitation of leading citizens on the topical question of
paration. After I had recorded all the evidence I ad-
urned the case till next day, when the Government
dvocate would be asked to address me on the law.

On reaching my chamber upstairs I found it littered
th bricks. I was now told that the crowd had become
mbroiled with the police, who had attempted to discipline
A violent flght had ensued, the crowd had been scat-
red, and there were many casualties. The hospital is full,
clerks told me.

As soon as Mr. Sen Gupta had left for the jail—there
s no-one to cheer him that afternoon—I set off for the
spital.

As I went along I picked up more information. The
eet outside my office was strewn with clubs, garments,
d bricks. The exterior of the court had a battered look
th its broken windows. Not an Indian was to be seen.
e police on duty seemed to be a fresh lot and could tell
little, but I gathered that the trouble had started by an
lian parading with a banner. The banner gave the crowd
herence and a sense of importance; the police had no
nner; the crowd began to despise the police. To show
ir contempt they pulled a mounted policeman off his
ny when he was attempting to interfere with the parade

like it, for it reflected upon his conduct of the case and relegated him for the time being to the position of a spectator.

'I am informed that the witnesses are present,' he replied,
in the manner of a man who desired to humour an eccentric judge.

Sen Gupta did not seem much better pleased. Though
the witnesses I was about to call were the very persons he
must have called had he desired to defend the case and
explain his actions, he assumed an air of utter indifference,
and taking from his friend, Mr. Sen, the first newspaper
that offered, buried himself in it, only emerging to draw
attention in a whisper to some item in the telegrams. He
was playing his part and I relished it very much. As a man
it was impossible for him to be otherwise than deeply
interested in what I was doing on his behalf; as a politician,
one of the leaders of a party which throve on imprisonments, he deplored the line he observed me to be taking.
The case against him was, in his opinion, such a monstrously poor one that a heavy sentence would make him
a martyr. As a man he did not want to go to prison; as a
politician he felt obliged to go, and because he was a brave
and devoted man in his own line his duty weighed with him
more strongly than his personal comfort. So he was excited
and disappointed at once. But all eyes were upon him; the
Press of half Asia was in the court-room; his supporters
were bellowing themselves hoarse in the street. He must
be careful, let not a sign escape him. I caught his glance
for a second and saw all the truth before he again bent
over his newspaper in apparent concentration.

The first witness was Swami Shyamananda, who three
months before had expressed himself so properly about
Sir Charles on the station platform. The Ramakrishna
Mission, of which he was the manager in Burma, maintained a hospital and was concerned with other works of
charity and the relief of suffering. In appearance the
Swami was venerable and mild, nor was his appearance

in the least at variance with his character. He was, as he looked, a saintly man, and was therefore the perfect defence witness.

'Did you hear either of Mr. Sen Gupta's speeches?' I asked, after he had taken the oath in an impressive manner.

'I intended to hear them both,' replied the Swami. 'I was most anxious to listen to what he had to tell us. On the 20th of February I tried to enter the Hurry Krishna Hall, but the crush was too great. Next morning, however, I was able to read in the newspapers what he had said, and it interested me so much that I went to his meeting in the afternoon at Fytche Square. Again the crowd was so thick that I could not get near enough to hear.'

That was what the Swami had to say, and as it was impossible to picture him struggling to hear a really seditious speech his evidence, slight though it was, had a certain weight.

The next witness was Mr. Paw Tun. He was telling me what the reader already knows—that he had been asked to preside at anti-separation meetings—when I heard a roar from the street far louder than the bursts of shouting which up to this point had followed the case. From my position on the bench I could see through some panes of glass on the upper part of the end doors and now perceived men running to and fro or jumping over the wall of the church compound. There was a sound of blows and of scurrying feet. It was evident that the demonstration was turning into something else, and a brick which struck the door and shattered the glass suggested that after all there was going to be an attack on the court.

Mr. Sen Gupta had put down his newspaper. While flattered that his supporters should take his arrest and trial so much to heart he was not wholly satisfied, for violence was dead against the Congress policy. But perhaps it might be turned to some account, for if it annoyed me into taking a more serious view of his case on the ground,

fallacious but possible, that his speeches ha crowd, that would be all to the good and n situation which was turning very flat.

Realizing this and determined that he sh encouragement I remarked at once with a neg

'The crowd seems to be in high spirits th remark which obliged him again to resort to h

Mr. Merrikin, who was sitting directly be bar, now caught my eye and by a sign indica going outside. Totally unarmed as he was, I for the door and disappear through it in bricks.

My place was on the bench and I resolve from it nor to adjourn the case as long a would reply to my questions. I was going to or whatever it was, hear nothing but M answers, see nothing but what his face and r and so discourage Sen Gupta from thinkin could deflect me from my intention of whole truth of his case.

I did not know what was happening out there was a fight going on and that the n the pile of bricks in the church compound ful. That was obvious, for the doors and court were continually struck by bricks a them falling on the floor of the chamber At this hot moment Mr. Tyabji left the c Mr. Merrikin and as unarmed. He had a going out, if it was at his behest that assembled. A firm believer in peaceful n tion for Indians, especially on this occ Indians were his men, he wanted to tell th ing, because as the affair stood he might fomenting a riot. But he was almost imme head with a brick and was carried insensi hospital.

like it, for it reflected upon his conduct of the case and relegated him for the time being to the position of a spectator.

'I am informed that the witnesses are present,' he replied, in the manner of a man who desired to humour an eccentric judge.

Sen Gupta did not seem much better pleased. Though the witnesses I was about to call were the very persons he must have called had he desired to defend the case and explain his actions, he assumed an air of utter indifference, and taking from his friend, Mr. Sen, the first newspaper that offered, buried himself in it, only emerging to draw attention in a whisper to some item in the telegrams. He was playing his part and I relished it very much. As a man it was impossible for him to be otherwise than deeply interested in what I was doing on his behalf; as a politician, one of the leaders of a party which throve on imprisonments, he deplored the line he observed me to be taking. The case against him was, in his opinion, such a monstrously poor one that a heavy sentence would make him a martyr. As a man he did not want to go to prison; as a politician he felt obliged to go, and because he was a brave and devoted man in his own line his duty weighed with him more strongly than his personal comfort. So he was excited and disappointed at once. But all eyes were upon him; the Press of half Asia was in the court-room; his supporters were bellowing themselves hoarse in the street. He must be careful, let not a sign escape him. I caught his glance for a second and saw all the truth before he again bent over his newspaper in apparent concentration.

The first witness was Swami Shyamananda, who three months before had expressed himself so properly about Sir Charles on the station platform. The Ramakrishna Mission, of which he was the manager in Burma, maintained a hospital and was concerned with other works of charity and the relief of suffering. In appearance the Swami was venerable and mild, nor was his appearance in the least at variance with his character. He was, as he looked, a saintly man, and was therefore the perfect defence witness.

'Did you hear either of Mr. Sen Gupta's speeches?' I asked, after he had taken the oath in an impressive manner.

'I intended to hear them both,' replied the Swami. 'I was most anxious to listen to what he had to tell us. On the 20th of February I tried to enter the Hurry Krishna Hall, but the crush was too great. Next morning, however, I was able to read in the newspapers what he had said, and it interested me so much that I went to his meeting in the afternoon at Fytche Square. Again the crowd was so thick that I could not get near enough to hear.'

That was what the Swami had to say, and as it was impossible to picture him struggling to hear a really seditious speech his evidence, slight though it was, had a certain weight.

The next witness was Mr. Paw Tun. He was telling me what the reader already knows—that he had been asked to preside at anti-separation meetings—when I heard a roar from the street far louder than the bursts of shouting which up to this point had followed the case. From my position on the bench I could see through some panes of glass on the upper part of the end doors and now perceived men running to and fro or jumping over the wall of the church compound. There was a sound of blows and of scurrying feet. It was evident that the demonstration was turning into something else, and a brick which struck the door and shattered the glass suggested that after all there was going to be an attack on the court.

Mr. Sen Gupta had put down his newspaper. While flattered that his supporters should take his arrest and trial so much to heart he was not wholly satisfied, for violence was dead against the Congress policy. But perhaps it might be turned to some account, for if it annoyed me into taking a more serious view of his case on the ground, fallacious but possible, that his speeches had roused the crowd, that would be all to the good and might rescue a situation which was turning very flat.

Realizing this and determined that he should have no encouragement I remarked at once with a negligent air:

'The crowd seems to be in high spirits this morning,' a remark which obliged him again to resort to his newspaper.

Mr. Merrikin, who was sitting directly below me at the bar, now caught my eye and by a sign indicated that he was going outside. Totally unarmed as he was, I saw him make for the door and disappear through it into the rain of bricks.

My place was on the bench and I resolved not to move from it nor to adjourn the case as long as Mr. Paw Tun would reply to my questions. I was going to ignore the riot or whatever it was, hear nothing but Mr. Paw Tun's answers, see nothing but what his face and manner told me, and so discourage Sen Gupta from thinking that anything could deflect me from my intention of laying bare the whole truth of his case.

I did not know what was happening outside, except that there was a fight going on and that the mob was finding the pile of bricks in the church compound extremely useful. That was obvious, for the doors and windows of the court were continually struck by bricks and I could hear them falling on the floor of the chamber above my head. At this hot moment Mr. Tyabji left the court, as small as Mr. Merrikin and as unarmed. He had a strong reason for going out, if it was at his behest that the crowd had assembled. A firm believer in peaceful methods of agitation for Indians, especially on this occasion, when the Indians were his men, he wanted to tell them to stop fighting, because as the affair stood he might be charged with fomenting a riot. But he was almost immediately hit on the head with a brick and was carried insensible to the general hospital.

I continued to the best of my ability amid the uproar and crashes to examine Mr. Paw Tun, who stood like a rock in the witness box, answering my questions with perfect lucidity. After I had dismissed him I examined in succession Captain Rushall, the Mayor of Rangoon, a true Conrad figure; Abdul Bari Chowdhury, the manager of the Bengal-Burma Steam Navigation Company; Mr. Pillai, who represented West Rangoon Indian Constituency; and a number of others. Their evidence, which became easier to hear as the noise of the riot died away in the distance, provided me with the complete picture of Mr. Sen Gupta's visit, and proved that his speeches had been delivered by invitation of leading citizens on the topical question of separation. After I had recorded all the evidence I adjourned the case till next day, when the Government Advocate would be asked to address me on the law.

On reaching my chamber upstairs I found it littered with bricks. I was now told that the crowd had become embroiled with the police, who had attempted to discipline it. A violent flght had ensued, the crowd had been scattered, and there were many casualties. The hospital is full, my clerks told me.

As soon as Mr. Sen Gupta had left for the jail—there was no-one to cheer him that afternoon—I set off for the hospital.

As I went along I picked up more information. The street outside my office was strewn with clubs, garments, and bricks. The exterior of the court had a battered look with its broken windows. Not an Indian was to be seen. The police on duty seemed to be a fresh lot and could tell me little, but I gathered that the trouble had started by an Indian parading with a banner. The banner gave the crowd coherence and a sense of importance; the police had no banner; the crowd began to despise the police. To show their contempt they pulled a mounted policeman off his pony when he was attempting to interfere with the parade

of the banner. When some of the Mogul Guard rushed
forward a volley of bricks was thrown, and the fight was
on. It had lasted an hour and there were eighty casualties.
So they told me. Nobody was killed. Mr. Merrikin had
escaped unhurt, as had his assistant, Mr. Barker, though
the latter sustained the loss of his umbrella, which he had
carried throughout the battle and the remains of which he
abandoned on the field.

I hurried on to the hospital. In the porch I met Sergeants
Pimley and Ryan. The former was limping, and Ryan had
a bandage round his head; he was very pale.

'Well, Ryan,' I said, 'are you hurt?'

'No, sir,' said he, cheerfully.

'What's that bandage, then?'

'He was struck above the eye with a brick,' said Pimley.

'Are there many of you damaged?' I asked.

'The Crown Sergeant was stabbed in the shoulder and
Hough in the head. And they clubbed Triggs and Crisp had
his arm hurt.'

'You seem to have been mauled,' I said. 'Did the
Indians get away with it?'

'They did not, sir,' said Ryan.

I saw one of the assistant doctors passing and beckoned
to him.

'How many Indians have come in for treatment?'

"About forty, sir.' He hurried on.

'But a lot more went to the Ramakrishna hospital and
to the dispensaries,' said Pimley. 'We warmed up the
bastards when we got them on the run.'

'I hit a few myself,' said Ryan reflectively.

'They'll be quiet to-morrow,' said Pimley.

'If there're any outside the court you won't hear a word
out of them,' said Ryan. 'And I hope, sir, that for this
you'll give that black b——'

'The case is *sub judice*, Ryan. While a trial's on you
mustn't try to influence the magistrate.'

'No, sir,' said Ryan, 'but I hope you'll give that black b——'

'That will do, Ryan.'

'Yes, sir.'

They went off. Ryan had a certain reputation in the force. After hitting a man he used to pick him up and shake hands with him. He had shaken hands with a lot of people in Rangoon.

6. THE DINNER PARTY

Sergeant Ryan's forecast was correct. The crowd outside the court next morning was small and silent. It looked at the building, at the strong force of police and military police concentrated upon it, and hardly raised a cheer when the prisoner arrived. Except for a man selling leaflets on which was printed a portrait of Sen Gupta there was no activity.

In this pleasant quiet I asked the Government Advocate to address me. Mr. Eggar was in a difficult position and he knew it. There were two courses open to him; to both of them there were objections. He could confine himself to his original brief, point to the letter of the speeches, and, declaring them to be seditious, call for a penalty. Or he could declare that though the evidence which I had insisted should be on record threw a fresh light upon the case and though the accused's object had now been shown to be the making of speeches on the political question of separation, he had overstepped the bounds of legitimate criticism and had used seditious words. The objection to the first course was that it could carry no weight, for it was impossible to ignore the new evidence; but to admit that

Sen Gupta's general intention was legitimate, though his words in places were such as to excite disaffection, was to water the case down till it became absurd that the Mayor of Calcutta should have been brought such a distance to answer so trifling an indictment.

Mr. Eggar was in a dilemma and he sought to circumvent it, as many another has done in a similar situation, by making a long speech, which occupied the whole morning.

So far as I could follow his argument, it seemed to me to stray from the established facts. Sen Gupta was represented as having landed with the intention of creating disaffection against the Government, the speeches he made being proof of that intention. They were not genuine well-argued speeches against separation, because they contained too many inaccuracies. Mr. Eggar pointed out the inaccuracies at length, exhibiting a knowledge of Burmese history and local affairs certainly much in advance of that Sen Gupta possessed. But the argument that slipshod dates and figures proved criminal intent hardly held my attention; I could not give it the consideration he thought it deserved, and found my mind frequently wandering.

He turned then to inquire why Sen Gupta had refused to plead. It was an admission of guilt, nothing less. Here I found myself in some agreement with the speaker. Sen Gupta had certainly hoped that his refusal to plead would be taken as equivalent to a plea of guilty. Unfortunately I could not tell Mr. Eggar that he was doing all he could to oblige the prisoner, whose object was to manœuvre me into passing upon him a heavy sentence for something he had not done.

Sen Gupta himself found the speech desperately dull. He did not yet know exactly what line I was going to take, whether I was about to discharge him or record a technical conviction, but he knew that his original hope of making big capital out of the case was gone. He might be able to laugh at the Burma Government, but he would not be able to charge it with grave injustice. Laughter was no good to Gandhi at that moment; one could not rouse the masses to heroic heights by making them laugh. Sacrifice could only be stimulated by a sense of bitter wrong, and there was now no chance of finding that stimulus in Rangoon. Earlier in the trial Sen Gupta's reading of newspapers had been a calculated affectation. Now he turned to them simply in order to be distracted. I envied him his licence.

When Mr. Eggar had finished I adjourned the case till Saturday, which gave me the following day in which to make up my mind and write my orders. I could either dis-charge Sen Gupta or, after framing a definite charge or charges against him, convict and sentence him for sedition. I was not yet sure which course was correct, though I knew that the sedition—if it existed—was of a technical nature.

That night I had arranged a dinner-party in my house. Two senior civilians and friends of mine were coming, Philip Fogarty and Bernard Swithinbank. I was glad they were coming, but I knew they could not help me. The general rule that a magistrate should not discuss a case he is trying is founded on good reason. No-one can properly advise him, for no-one but himself has heard all the evi-dence and studied the demeanour of the witnesses. The most that any friend can do is to draw his attention to accepted interpretations of the law. I had a friend who had quietly given me such assistance, but now I stood alone and had to make my decision alone with the facts. Yet it was pleasant to feel that Fogarty and Swithinbank were coming. If they could not help me their friendship could sustain me. They understood exactly how I was situated. Chance might have put either of them in my position and both of them had had in their experience similar problems to solve. Meeting daily all sorts of people in the course of their work or at the clubs, they had heard what was being said up and down Rangoon. They knew the executive's state of mind, the surprise and annoyance caused by the calling of the additional witnesses. They fully appreciated how exceedingly awkward it all was for those who had launched the prosecution; nor were they indifferent to the comedy which underlay the proceedings.

My guests began to arrive at a quarter-past eight. It was the hot weather. The sun had set that evening in a haze of dust. Even at eight-thirty the temperature was about 80° F. The electric fans were swinging in the ceiling and, imprisoned in a starched shirt, I felt the sweat running down my back. Yet as the guests came in there was not a tired or gloomy face. The Sen Gupta trial had enlivened them all. It had been so full of incident, it was such a human drama. Everyone was puzzled to know what I was going to do, and, if I let off Sen Gupta, what the Government would do to me. Rumours of every kind had kept the town amused. It was said that I had been at school with Sen Gupta; that Mr. Tyabji had been hit on the head not by a stray brick, but by Sergeant Ryan; that the Government of India had ordered the Burma Government to arrest Sen Gupta; that if I discharged Sen Gupta, Sir Charles would resign or, alternatively, that I should be sacked. It resulted that all the protagonists of the drama, Sen Gupta, Sir Charles, myself, with Mr. Eggar, Mr. Merrikin, right down to Sergeant Ryan, had acquired a notoriety which, according to the company, became a popularity or its reverse, but which in any case made us more interesting than we were before. Such mild excitements help the bored exile to remember without nostalgia the English winds of March and the bus traffic in Regent Street where it debouches into Piccadilly Circus.

In these favourable circumstances the dinner-party was a great success. Laughter was incessant, the conversation was sparkling. Sen Gupta, who was a man with a strong sense of humour, would have enjoyed it very much had it been possible for him to be present, but though his trial was a remarkable one it had not quite reached that point of

farce where the accused could dine with the trying magistrate. That touch was to be reserved for a later case, as
sensational as Sen Gupta's and as full of comedy, where
the criminal and myself were to dance together at Government House.

After dinner I was in the hall with Fogarty and Swithinbank, showing them my Chinese porcelains, which did not
interest them, and seeing that their thirst was frequently
quenched.

'What are you going to do?' Fogarty could not help
asking me at last.

The question brought me back to unwelcome earth. 'I
haven't yet made up my mind,' I said, the thought of the
morrow's heavy responsibility clouding over me.

'Let him off. It will please lots of people.' Philip was in
high spirits; he was hounding on the gladiators.

Swithinbank smiled. Rugged and severe, he looked at
Philip with indulgence; a distinguished man, upright and a
great scholar, he disliked the footlights, but he was too
intelligent to be insensible to the occasion.

I turned to him. 'What do you think, Bernard?'

'I don't know. I can't know. But get the law right, if you
can, and don't bother about the hullabaloo.'

The guests left me towards midnight. When the last car
had swung out of the gate I stood in the garden breathing
the dark air. The house was not far from some monasteries,
where an occasional sweet bell sounded, late though it was,
and from the bamboos on my right came the jingle of Burmese music. Over all floated the great pagoda, floodlit
against the stars. But Sen Gupta was asleep in his cell; it
was time for me also to rest. I told them to shut the doors
and, tired out, went to bed.

7. I MAKE UP MY MIND

Next day, when my ordinary file was disposed of, I turned my whole attention to the decision I had to make. The reader may feel that I have already indicated what that decision was bound to be, but in point of fact I was still in doubt. From the first I had perceived that the case was a border-line case, and sometimes I thought it fell on one side and sometimes on the other side of the border. But studying afresh the section and the rulings I saw that my first impression was right and that almost any disagreeable remark aimed at the Government might be held to be an attempt to bring it into hatred and contempt or to excite disaffection towards it, certainly as far as the subject in question was concerned. Sen Gupta had made certain disagreeable remarks and inevitably, therefore, what he had said was over the border-line.

I went through the speeches again with the object of selecting one or two of the worst expressions, so that I could incorporate them into definite charges. In his first speech in Fytche Square he had stated that it was not his intention to criticize the Government of Burma as the established government, but as the government which had advocated separation. He declared that the Congress policy of non-separation was the only one which could give Burma and India what they, both wanted, namely a free government. So far, so good; there was nothing seditious there nor had he been prosecuted on account of the first speech.

In the second speech, in the Hurry Krishna Hall, he had repeated the same argument, but in the course of his re-marks had told the students present that, inasmuch as the Government discouraged them from studying politics, it

was afraid, 'as men of sin are always afraid of truth'. He
called the Government 'men of sin' and went on to say
that they spied on the private life of the students, as they
did on everyone else, with their C.I.D. detectives. When
he said these words there were C.I.D. detectives in the
room, pencil in hand, and he knew it. But that made no
difference to the fact that the words were seditious, for
they attempted to disaffect the students and to decry not
separation as a policy but the existing form of Government. 'Men of sin' was the worst phrase I could find and I
extracted it to copy into the charge.

In the third speech the argument as a whole was concerned with the admitted object of his visit, but again he
overstepped the latitude given by the law to express disap-
probation of a measure and used words likely to cause
disaffection when he accused the Government of having
kept troops inside the precincts of the Shwedagon Pagoda,
as Cromwell had in churches. The Government had in fact
kept troops there for nearly a hundred years and had only
evacuated the place a few months before his visit. But for
him to say, 'How could any Burman think of tolerating
the rule of a nation which committed sacrilege of the most
sacred place of the people they profess to govern?' was to
utter seditious words. Then he went on—'Why did they
evacuate the pagoda?'—and gave the answer—'Because of
public opinion,' adding that the same public opinion could
oblige the English to evacuate the whole country, to the
occupation of which they had no more moral right than
to the occupation of the pagoda. 'But', he continued, 'your
public opinion alone will not be strong enough to get the
English out of Burma, you must have the support of the
suffering non-violent martyrs of India, because the British
have built at enormous expense a new cantonment for
their troops outside Rangoon and with these troops they
calculate to hold you in subjection for ever. When His
Excellency tells you that these troops are to protect you

against invasion from India or China an evil spirit is speaking in him.'

It was true that a new cantonment had been built to house as many British troops as were deemed necessary to safeguard the Government from dangers, internal and external, but to draw attention in such a way to what was a normal charge upon the public funds was in a literal sense seditious. I therefore extracted that passage also and set it in the charge. Sen Gupta clearly had been in somewhat of a quandary. He had been asked by Indians with capital sunk in Burma to persuade the Burmese that it was safer to rely on Indian than on English promises. How could he do that except by comparing the latter unfavourably with the former? But to say, when the Government was English, that one should believe an Indian sooner than an Englishman was to come dangerously near to technical sedition; to give reasons for such a view, to cite instances where the actions of the Government set up by the English conflicted, really or apparently, with their protestations, was certainly to go over the line. So when Sen Gupta accepted Abdul Bari Chowdhury's invitation to speak on the subject of separation, from the Congress point of view, he was bound to utter sedition. If he said nothing objectionable about the Government he would have given the Burmans no reason for preferring Gandhi, and his speech would have had about as much appeal to a popular audience as a leading article in *The Times*. But that did not excuse what he had said and make it legally innocuous.

So I argued to myself on that 22nd of March, the thermometer standing in the region of ninety, and signed the charge sheet containing the two extracts. As Sen Gupta would not plead to the charges I should have to pass sentence immediately afterwards. What was the right sentence?

The right sentence appeared to me the sentence which is passed for a technical offence. A small fine would have been applicable, but Sen Gupta would not pay a fine. It was therefore more sensible to sentence him to a short term of imprisonment without labour. The minimum term possible was imprisonment till the rising of the court, a sentence analogous to a farthing's damages. But there was something in the case, after all. Sen Gupta had broken the law, and though its machinery had seldom been set in motion for so slight a breach, I thought the number of days' imprisonment which corresponded to a small fine was the right sentence. I fixed it at ten days and wrote out my judgement at length.

It was approaching midnight when this was done. As I affixed my signature a great relief came over me. I was rid of all doubt now, certain that I had interpreted the law correctly. So closely had my mind been occupied with this task that I had forgotten the Government and how my judgement would read from an executive point of view. In this happy state I put away the papers, switched off the light, and went upstairs.

8. SEN GUPTA SMILES

Next morning early I re-read my judgement, but did not alter a word. I was satisfied that it would stand the scrutiny of the High Court. At ten o'clock I was on my way down to my office. On entering Montgomery Street I saw that the crowd was again very large. Mr. Merrikin this time had piled up the guards. Besides an ample force of city police, military police lined the footpaths opposite the entrance of the court and occupied the compound of the Rangoon Catholic Church.

At 10.45 I saw from my window Sen Gupta arriving with his escort. There was not a sound from the crowd. Silently they watched him pass into the building. At eleven o'clock precisely I took my seat on the bench. The first person I noticed was Mr. Tyabji, and he was very noticeable, for his head was swathed completely in bandages, on top of which he wore the white cap. I was delighted to see him on his feet again so soon, and though the etiquette of the bench prevented me from addressing a remark to a spectator I caught his eye for the fraction of a second.

Mr. Eggar looked up at me sourly and apprehensively. He had no idea what was coming. Sen Gupta was equally puzzled. As a lawyer he knew well enough that he had just overstepped the law, but I believe he thought that I was going to discharge him. The sole question for him was, what capital he could make out of the affair, and there was precious little to be made out of it if he was not going to prison. His friends in India had not been able publicly to criticize his arrest because the matter was *sub judice*, but they had turned the riot to account, stating that the Burma police had brutally assaulted a crowd of orderly spectators and driven them with many casualties from the court door. Mr. Munshi, who represented a Burma constituency in the Legislative Assembly at Delhi, had already tabled no less than twenty-two questions. He told the House that, in addition to the police, troops had been called out and that 'the use of troops against a non-violent crowd was a wanton display of brute force'. In short, they were all doing their best, but there was wretchedly little in it, and to eke it out they had to prevaricate about the troops. But if Sen Gupta were convicted and heavily sentenced they would have enough ammunition for a long bombardment. Such a conviction would be the real stuff so hard to stage, a genuine exhibition of high-handedness.

I addressed myself to Mr. Sen Gupta. 'Early in the trial you said you were not prepared to answer any questions?'

'Yes,' replied Mr. Sen Gupta, and then suddenly perceived that he had answered a question.

'Very well, I am now going to charge you,' and I read out the two charges I had framed, quoting words he had used and declaring that they were seditious words.

I then said: 'Am I to understand that you do not wish to plead to these charges?'

Mr. Sen Gupta was not going to be caught again with a 'yes'. He should logically, of course, have remained silent with the appropriate expression of the man who refuses to recognize the right of the tyrant to judge him, but as his case had been tried with such abounding, if inconvenient, fairness, his sense of humour prevented him from adopting so idiotic a pose, and he muttered something about being unable to answer any questions.

I then read out my judgement, which occupied half an hour, and sentenced him to the ten days' simple imprisonment. When he heard the sentence he smiled. That was to be the cue. The whole nationalist Press would be told to smile. The case had failed to produce a martyrdom, but there was good material in it for laughing at the Government, at least at the executive side. But they could not laugh at the British nation, for the court which had tried the case was a British court, presided over by a British magistrate. The less said about that the better.

So Mr. Sen Gupta smiled. Yet, as he was a human being as well as a politician, there was a little more in his smile than policy. He was genuinely relieved that he had not to go to prison for six months or a year in a foreign jail eight hundred miles away from his wife and children. And he smiled, too, because his heart was warmed. Opponent though he was of British rule in India, his heart had been won against his judgement by the way he had been tried. For underneath everything he had a soft and affectionate heart, and he was as near weeping as smiling when he heard his sentence.

The court rose immediately. Sen Gupta went with his escort into the ante-room at the foot of the stairs leading to my chamber. I saw him there in animated conversation with the leading Indian gentlemen of Rangoon. On emerging from the court buildings by the side door he was asked to pose by the Press photographers. He did so for a moment and then entered the police car, into which one of his admirers had thrown a garland of flowers. 'In order to satisfy the curiosity of the spectators on the streets,' stated the *Rangoon Gazette* next day,' the Commissioner of Police ordered the car to drive past the crowds, and on this being done the spectators cheered Mr. Sen Gupta on his way to the central jail.'

I am inclined to doubt whether Mr. Merrikin ever gave such an order. He came upstairs with me to my chamber and we leaned out of the window together, saw Sen Gupta pass, heard the cheers, remarked the waving mob, the lances of the police. Mr. Merrikin looked tired and worn; it had been a heavy strain, the riot and anxiety. And already in his blood was the malignant poison which was to kill him the following year.

As Sen Gupta disappeared into the distance I ventured: 'Well, it's over now.'

But he was depressed and said: 'Ten days seems very little.'

To him Sen Gupta appeared a flaunting rebel, as indeed he was from a purely executive point of view.

Merrikin departed and I decided to go round at once to the Secretariat and see the executive in the persons of Mr. Lloyd, the Chief Secretary, and Sir J. A. Maung Gyi, the Home Member. As my judgement had amounted to a severe slap in the face for them I thought I had better present myself without delay.

Ten minutes later I entered Mr. Lloyd's room. Sir J. A. Maung Gyi was leaning over his shoulder. They were looking at papers on the desk in front of them, and as I came forward stared at me with uneasiness.

'I have convicted Sen Gupta,' I said abruptly.

'Oh,' they said with evident relief.

I heard afterwards that the papers before them related to an application to the High Court. They thought I was going to discharge Sen Gupta and were preparing to approach the High Court at once.

'And I have sentenced him to ten days' simple imprisonment,' I added.

There was silence. This part of my statement was not nearly so satisfactory as the first part.

Finally Mr. Lloyd said: 'I've been looking up the old cases, and I don't remember seeing a sentence of that length.'

The answer to that remark was clear. 'If ten days has never been given for sedition, a case as weak as Sen Gupta's has never previously been taken before a court.' But I could hardly say this to the officials who shared the responsibility for the prosecution. Accordingly I replied, mildly: 'I think, sir, when you have read my judgement, and the evidence upon which it is founded, that you will agree that a longer sentence was not possible.'

With that I took leave to withdraw.

I do not know what the Government thought when they read the judgement, but they must have been advised that an application to the High Court to enhance the sentence was unlikely to succeed, for they accepted my view by taking no action to get it altered. Nor do I know whether Sir Charles was annoyed or not. He had every reason to be annoyed, but he never showed it. In this he was actuated by the highest motives. To India and to the world at this trying moment when, as I shall point out, the Press of a whole continent was abusing him, he exhibited a great example of English virtue. He was not in good health, and his nerves had suffered in consequence. Yet the attitude, which he consistently maintained, was an extraordinary illustration of the propriety with which the English submit to the rule of law.

9. THE UPROAR

The next day, Sunday, 23 March, the uproar in the Press began. The *Rangoon Mail* and the *Rangoon Daily News*, both Indian-owned papers, headed it with two leading articles. They were obliged to admit that the court which had given Sen Gupta a fair trial was English, but they made great play with the executive for having instituted the prosecution. What a wonderful advertisement it had given Mr. Sen Gupta and his ideas on separation! The Government could not have found a better way of strengthening the case of those who were opposed to them on that question.

On the Tuesday following a meeting was held in Fytche Square, and was attended by Burmans as well as Indians. The newspapers were right, the anti-separationists had been strengthened. The monks and women, who had avoided the trial after their disappointment on the wharf, again appeared. U Ba Si, a Burman politician, was voted into the chair. A number of Bunnans, including Dr. Thein Maung, who to-day is Minister for Commerce and Industry, made speeches. U Ba Si and Dr. Thein Maung were separationists, but they said a lot of agreeable things to the Indians on that occasion. A better feeling was momentarily established between the two races, and as to the anti-separationist Bunnans, their increased influence dates from that day. The Government was, of course, roundly abused; but on a long view the sting was taken out of what was said by the tributes simultaneously paid to British justice.

During the ensuing days the Indian Press got to work. The *Leader* of Allahabad said that the Government of Burma had 'erred egregiously'. The *Amrit Bazaar Patrika* of Calcutta said: '. . . if the Burma Government wanted to earn universal ridicule, it has succeeded.' It also remarked significantly and with more truth, perhaps, than it intended: 'Mr. Sen Gupta went to Rangoon prepared for the worst. He certainly did not expect the cheap martyrdom thus thrust upon him.' A number of leading Indians of moderate politics were asked to express their views. Pandit Kunzru, a Liberal, said the Government 'could not have chosen a better way of bringing law into contempt', and Raja Ghazanfarali declared: 'Looking at the evidence produced before the court and the way Mr. Sen Gupta was arrested and taken to Burma one considers the whole affair was a huge joke. It is hardly necessary to say that the Burma Government's reputation has not improved by this farce.' Even the great Mr. Gandhi himself found time, in the midst of his preparations for the march to the sea coast, to turn the episode to good account in an article in *Young India*. He said that had I been living in an envirpnment of freedom I would have discharged Sen Gupta and reprimanded the Government for bringing a frivolous complaint. He also declared: 'If disaffection is a crime and Section 124A has any reality about it I, who made of sedition a religion, should have been tried and heavily punished long ago. But the Government is afraid in the face of world opinion; the policy of non-violent revolution is right; victory in the near future is certain.'

Finally I must quote the *Statesman*, the leading organ of the English community in India, which in a few words unmasked the inner meaning of the case. 'At least one of their martyrdoms has been a dismal failure. Having regard to the charge and evidence brought against him in Rangoon, we may think that a sentence of ten days' imprisonment was ample for Mr. Sen Gupta. But it must have been a grievous disappointment to him.'

The newspapers representing English interests in Rangoon—the *Gazette* and *The Times*—made no editorial comments, though they reported the case verbatim. They were the only newspapers in the whole Empire of India which might have said a healing word for the Burma Government, but they said nothing.

This spate of criticism, the volume of which makes Sir Charles Innes's restraint all the more admirable, was not confined to the Press. It invaded the legislature. I have already alluded to Mr. Munshi's twenty-two questions, which were tabled when the case was *sub judice.* The termination of the trial was his moment and he returned to the assault.

On the 31st of March there was a lively scene at New Delhi. It was question time in the Legislative Assembly. Mr. Haig (he has been knighted since, I am glad to say) was the acting Home Member of Council. Being a Civilian he had had no more parliamentary experience than other Civilians, and on that day was cruelly heckled by Mr. Munshi and other tried politicians, including the formidable old Pandit Malaviya. They wanted to get at the reason for Sen Gupta's arrest.

'Did the Government of Burma first consult the Government of India?'

'Yes.'

'Did the Government of India sanction the prosecution after examining the papers?'

'The Government of India has not seen the papers.'

'Why, in that case, did they sanction the prosecution?'

'They did not sanction it, they were only told about it.'

'Who was responsible, then, for the prosecution?'

'The initiative came entirely from the Government of Burma, on whom the responsibility for deciding on the prosecution lies.'

'Why did the Government of India allow them to prosecute?'

'They had the right to institute such a prosecution in their territory.'

'If so, why did they consult the Government of India?'

'To be sure that they were acting in accordance with the Government of India's views.'

'Is the Government of India's view the same as that expressed by the Viceroy on 25 January, when he said prosecution for sedition would be confined to cases where violence was inculcated or where a speech was incidental to a movement directed to the subversion of law and the authority of the Government?'

'Yes.'

'Were Mr. Sen Gupta's speeches of that kind.'

'Yes.'

'How can the Government tell if they have never read them?'

'The Government of Burma would not have taken a course at variance with the Viceroy's policy.'

'Has the Government read the evidence given in court and the magistrate's judgement?'

'No.'

So it went on, member after member rising to bait Mr. Haig, who did remarkably well considering the kind of case he had to defend. At last Mr. Gayaprasad Singh asked: 'Does the Hon. Member realize that the Government of Burma and the Government of India have made themselves thoroughly ridiculous by the way in which they have prosecuted Mr. Sen Gupta?' At which point the President was obliged to interpose with, 'Order, Order.'

It would be interesting to know what was said in the lobbies that day.

The people who heckled Mr. Haig were, of course, political opponents of the Government and were making all the use they could of what for them was a happy windfall. I have been unable to quote the opinion of an impartial observer, for nobody of that description made a pronouncement at the time, nor did any apologist for the Government venture into print. But on behalf of the

Government of Burma it might have been urged in explanation that what had happened was something of the following nature. C.I.D. detectives under routine instructions took down Sen Gupta's speeches and submitted them to the head of their department, and he laid them before the Chief Secretary. There had been very little sedition talked in Burma, except of the straightforward blatant type, and the Chief Secretary was not accustomed to the kind of politico-seditious speeches which were being made every day all over India at that time. The insinuations against the Governor sounded to him worse than they would have sounded to a more experienced officer, and, after taking the Government Advocate's advice, which was too narrowly legal to be much guide as to the enormity of the offence, he submitted the papers to the Governor-in-Council with the recommendation that a prosecution be sanctioned.

Sir Charles Innes was irritated. Why, on top of all his other worries, must he put up with touring agitators from India? Without reflecting sufficiently that on a broad view and in their context the speeches could hardly be called 'incidental to a movement directed to the subversion of law and the authority of the Government', and still less were an attempt to incite to violence, he told the Council that Sen Gupta should be put before a magistrate and 'given the law'. In the circumstances, where their chief had been personally abused in the speeches, the two councillors, one of whom was a Burman, were disinclined to express a contrary opinion. The Government of India was then informed, more out of courtesy, because the accused was a prominent resident of another province, than for any rule of procedure. The Government of India had neither the time nor the inclination to do the Government of Burma's work, and, assuming that there were solid grounds for the prosecution, they replied that they had no objection to raise. Fortified by their approval, which in fact was worthless, the Governor-in-Council sanctioned the prosecution.

No explanation of this kind could have been put forward in print at the time, but many guessed that this was probably the course which events had taken.

As I read the newspaper comments on the trial and their accounts of the scene in the Legislative Assembly in Delhi the extreme delicacy of my own position became increasingly clear to me. I was the man who only a few months before had annoyed the mercantile community by taking the view that one of their employees had shown a lack of sensibility in his dealings with the Burmese. For that I was declared to be anti-English, though the views I had expressed would have been platitudes in England. Now again, in a case where the accused person was an oriental and notoriously an opponent of the form of government then existing in India, I had been obliged by the logic of facts to take his side against the executive. I could not help perceiving, with disagreeable plainness, that the prejudice, already created against me in the minds of some English residents of Rangoon by the first case, would be greatly extended by the second. While it could not be denied that Sen Gupta's sentence was correct enough in law, there would be many to argue that prestige was even more important than a correct interpretation of the law. How was prestige to be maintained if in the name of law judgements were passed which reinforced those vowed to destroy it?

I repeated this argument to myself, and saw that it was more likely to be generally accepted in Rangoon than the truth, which was that both judgements had increased our prestige by showing that the courts administered the law in the manner in which it was administered in England.

The law of England is admired the world over, and it is on the excellence of its practice that our moral right to be in India is founded. To meddle with it in the stress of political temper is to meddle with our greatest asset. Living in England safely now, after these trials, I rejoice in the constant proof that there are thousands in these islands who would have done exactly as I did; but I ask permission to tell them that they have escaped a great deal of unpleasantness through never having been obliged to try Sen Gupta.

10. SEN GUPTA'S FAREWELL

On the fourth day of Sen Gupta's imprisonment I went to the jail, of which I was an official visitor. My intention was to make my usual monthly inspection and at the same time to see how Sen Gupta was lodged. Lieut.-Colonel Flowerdew, of the Indian Medical Service, was the superintendent, a man much liked by the convicts, and who ruled the jail kindly and well.

I have a particular loathing for prisons, of which I have had to inspect a large number. There is a nauseating smell in them, and I do not know whether I smell it only through the nostrils. On that day, however, I felt less oppressed with horror than usual, for to see Sen Gupta would be an interesting change from the condemned cells and the wretchedness of the under-trial ward.

I think my inspection must have been a little perfunctory, for I seemed to reach very quickly the European ward, where Sen Gupta was confined. It was a large double-storied brick building. I was conducted upstairs into a long gallery, down both sides of which were cells with doors of bars. Some European and Eurasian convicts were there, making material for rope from the husk of coconuts. About three-quarter way down on the right-hand side I came to a cell with a curtain over the door.

'Mr. Sen Gupta,' respectfully called the chief jailer, an old Mohammedan, 'the District Magistrate would like to speak to you.'

The curtain was drawn aside and Sen Gupta came out with Lamb's *Essays* in his hand. We sat down in the corridor on two deck-chairs and the chief jailer arranged a portable fan so that it played directly over us.

'I see they have made you as comfortable as possible,' I said, 'but what about the food?'

One must begin a conversation somehow.

'The chief jailer has been attentive,' replied Sen Gupta, at which compliment the old man murmured deprecatingly: 'We're doing what we can, sir.'

Whether he was 'sirring' me or Sen Gupta I could not gather.

'What do you think of the place?' I asked the prisoner. The conversation halted a bit.

'For me quite restful for a week or so, but may I draw your attention to the man opposite?'

I looked across and saw a Eurasian youth called Pollard, who had stolen, I remembered, fifty thousand cigarettes and whom I had sent to prison for nine months with hard labour. His hands were bleeding; stripping the coconuts had torn them, as he was only accustomed to office work.

I expostulated with the chief jailer. 'If Mr. Sen Gupta— that is to say, if your Honour wishes—we can put him on to lighter work,' he hastened to reply.

The conversation languished again. At last Sen Gupta, breaking through the restraint, said: 'I'm to be released on Sunday night, I believe, and hope to leave Rangoon at dawn on Tuesday by the mail. May I come and say good-bye to you at your house on Monday evening?'

'Why yes, of course!'

'About nine o'clock? I want to thank you for——' he broke off.

I decided that it was time to continue my inspection, motioned to the chief jailer, and went on my way.

On Sunday afternoon Sen Gupta was released by order of the Government, though he had served only eight days of his sentence. He went to stay, I believe, with Mr. Sen, the lawyer, whose brother was Mr. Justice Sen of the High Court of Rangoon. On Monday afternoon he addressed a meeting again in Fytche Square and repeated the arguments of his former speeches, being careful, however, to be quite colourless. In the course of his remarks he alluded to the way his case had been tried and insinuated that persons like myself were a serious danger to the Congress movement.

That evening after dinner I heard a car drive up to my door and knew he had come. He left his shawl outside, and enormous, in brimming spirits, entered the drawing-room.

'What will you have to drink?' I asked, as he sat down on the sofa. It was a stifling night.

'When you saw me first,' he laughed, 'you offered me a cup of tea. I refused it, though you see I remember. May I have a glass of barley-water?'

It was brought, and he said: 'This afternoon I was abusing you in Fytche Square.'

'What did you say?'

'I said that judgements like yours are no good to us. They cramp our style.'

This hurt me a trifle, because he had not been frank enough to admit publicly his fair trial, because he had thought it necessary to laugh at what had nearly made him weep.

He saw my expression and abandoned his jocular air.

'I had to speak to the crowd like that. You see, in six days Gandhi begins non-violent civil disobedience. We are all to break the salt laws. Thousands of us will go to prison. I could not praise British justice at the very moment when we want to prove that it does not exist.'

'Will *you* have to go to prison again?'

He sighed. 'I shall be scarcely home before I am arrested once more.'

For a moment a sense of futility overcame me. 'It was hardly worth my while bothering about your trial here.'

He became serious. 'That was worth doing, whatever happens.'

'You tell me that and yet you go back to Bengal and to prison. Why was it worth doing?'

'Because it lies beyond the moment. I can say that here in this room, but outside I dare not be so frank. There, it is a battle of words, of wits. We cannot afford generous words, nor give any truth to the other side. A word lost is like a battalion lost. Had I said boldly in Fytche Square to-day that I had had a fair and open trial I should have been as incompetent as a diplomatist who blurts out the truth!'

I was depressed. 'It is a vast racket.'

'I am in no racket. I want nothing for myself, I believe in freedom and I admire justice. The way you tried me was admirable. But I have had bitter experiences. It is not enough to suffer and to speak the truth. To achieve freedom one has to act, and the tactics we now employ are the only tactics for an unarmed people.'

'You said just now of this trial—"it lies beyond the moment". What did you mean by that?'

'I meant that whatever Congress may say or do cannot touch it.' He smiled. 'You've won.'

Saying this, he got up from the sofa and stood looking vaguely at the room. 'I start for Bengal at dawn. No sooner there, I am caught up in the struggle. I may not see you again.'

'You have been very generous,' I said, 'and this is an unusual occasion. To mark it, will you take a small token from me?'

'I do not require a token to remember it.'

'But yet I will force you to take something from me. If I have won, you must acknowledge it by accepting my present.'

He laughed very loud at this, so. loud that my wife, who was upstairs, was sure he had woken the baby.

'What do you want to give me?'

I took up from my collection a small lion of white jade, a lion whose tail became a lotus blossom—a symbolic carving—and gave it to him. He placed it in a pocket over his heart. '"But it is time to close," he quoted lightly, "night's wheels are rattling fast over me—it is proper to have done with this solemn mockery." I must go—good-bye—in happier times perhaps——'

He went for his shawl. The car was in the porch and he climbed in. 'Good-bye,' he called again from the back seat and signed to the driver.

As he had said, within a few weeks of landing at Calcutta he was in prison again, with Gandhi and all the other leaders and with more than fifty thousand of the rank and file.

Nineteen months later, on the 10th of November 1931, when I was on leave in England, I had occasion to meet some friends at Victoria Station. At five o'clock a boat train came in. As the passengers went to the Customs I saw a familiar figure in the murk.

'Sen Gupta!'

He turned round. We shook hands. He had come in connection with the Round Table Conference. We exchanged a few words and he disappeared in a taxi.

I never saw him again. After the conference he was arrested as he landed at Bombay, in the last drive against the Congress. Worn out, his health shattered, he died not long afterwards.

CHAPTER FIVE

1. THE EARTHQUAKE

Gandhi's march to the sea began on the 6th of April, a week after the events described in the last chapter. The non-violent campaign which followed convulsed India, but it had no apparent reaction in Burma. Politicians, indeed, realized that its success would facilitate their task later on in London; the Indians were acting as shock troops and making a path which others could follow. Far-seeing Burmans understood this very well and knew that they were much beholden to Gandhi. But the national spirit in Burma, which was the counterpart of what was driving the Indians to offer themselves for imprisonment, paradoxically set the Burmese against the Indians, who were foreigners like the English and the Chinese. Many Indians in Burma were prosperous and influential, and not all the sufferings of their compatriots in India for the general cause of freedom could make the word 'Indian' sound sweeter in Burmese ears.

The Burma Government knew that a national spirit was about, but had no clue to the way in which it might manifest itself. The outward scene was reassuring. The hot-weather festivals were thronged as usual with laughing men and women. Officials were inclined to sit back and pity their hard-worked colleagues across the bay. In the past the Burmans had shown themselves easy-going people. Why should they not remain engaging, cheerful, and polite?

On 5 May Gandhi was arrested. The news was received in Rangoon during the late afternoon and the Indians immediately shut their shops. The Burmese did nothing; their eyes said nothing.

At 8.15 that evening I was walking in the moonlight when my consciousness began to waver. I staggered, my knees seemed to sag under me, and I felt suddenly sick. Stumbling and lurching I realized at last what was wrong —the ground was heaving under me in long waves.

The earthquake passed as quickly as it had come. Immediately I heard loud shouts from the houses within earshot. At that instant in the town many people were killed and injured, many buildings fell, the jewelled finial of the great Shwedagon Pagoda toppled sideways. In the panic a mob of Indians ran stoning those in their way and crying in triumph, 'Victory to the Holy Gandhi!'

Next morning the full extent of the damage was known. Rangoon had escaped comparatively lightly, but the old capital, Pegu, was almost totally destroyed. The casualties were heavy, but the English inhabitants had been lucky. At 8.15 p.m. the majority of them were sitting on the lawn outside their local club, gulping drinks and complaining of the heat. The stillness was remarkable; not a dog barked, the insects were hushed. There was not the smallest breath of air and, though out of doors, everyone felt as stifled as in a closed room. The moonlight was intense and the bulk of the Shwemawdaw Pagoda, a shrine nearly equal in reputation to the Shwedagon, loomed up enormously beyond the club grounds. Suddenly there was a deafening crash and the pagoda was rent, a large part of it crashing down. The English were flung from their chairs on to the ground. Terrified, they hurried home through the ruins of the town.

The earthquake was not connected by the Bunnans with the arrest of Gandhi, but was held to be a sure sign that tumultuous events were on the way. They were going to be masters again in their own house. Indians would have to be careful; if they wished to remain in Burma they would have to put Burma first. As for the other intruders, the

English, their time was coming too. So the whole Burmese nation believed. The educated class knew that the English could not be thrown out; their hope lay in constitutional agitation. But the country people counted on force; they had a vision of a conquering king. According to their secret prophetic books the English would begin to go after a hundred years. The hundred years were up, for Rangoon had fallen in 1825. Great events were surely close and the earthquake was a prelude to them.

2. THE MASSACRE

At 10 a.m. on 26 May my telephone rang.

'Hello?'

'Mr. Pillai speaking.'

Mr. Pillai was the Indian Member of the Burma Legislative Council, who had been one of the witnesses in the Sen Gupta trial. He was speaking from my office.

'What is it, Mr. Pillai?'

'The Burmese are killing the Indians.'

'Have you communicated with the police?'

'Yes, but the police won't do anything. The whole city is in the hands of the mob. Please come down.'

'I shall come down at once, but I am not in charge of the police.'

'You will be able to do something for us, sir. Hundreds of Indians have been killed and the massacre is continuing.'

This was very startling news. I had no idea why the Burmese had turned on the Indians and it was clearly my duty to find out immediately. Mr. Merrikin was solely responsible for police measures, but the Government would expect a report from me. I hurried out to my car. To get in touch with Mr. Merrikin was the first essential.

In the region of the Secretariat I ran into the turmoil. There a street fight was in progress between a band of Indian dock labourers and some Burmans of the lower class. The Burmans retreated into the Secretariat compound. Five or six policemen were standing about, but the rioters paid no attention to them, nor did they on their part attempt to interfere.

I found this a puzzling sight. Mr. Pillai's talk of massacre seemed beside the mark, and why were the policemen doing nothing? I spoke to one of them.

'We can't do anything,' he said. 'The whole city is like this, or, rather, much worse. It's only a skirmish here.'

'What's it all about?'

'I don't know.'

Impatiently I slipped in the gear-lever and moved on down the street. Round the corner I saw a sight which made me pause. A stout Burman dressed only in a skirt was painting signs on another Burman's chest. A number of others appeared to be awaiting their turn. This was very ominous. The signs were magical signs, and I knew that they were being painted on to give invulnerability. Before Burmans of the country class went into a fight they always paid a magician to make them bullet or sword-proof. It was generally done secretly, but here on the pavement was a magician hard at work. As I watched, a bus-load of Burmans arrived and called out to him. The fee was fourpence. He was doing a brisk trade. It signified a fight to the death, a fanatical, savage, mystical onslaught.

The Burmans paid no attention to me, nor was I in any position to cope with them.

A few minutes later I was at Mr. Merrikin's office in Dalhousie Street. The place seemed nearly empty, but I found a junior sub-inspector and told him I wanted to see the Commissioner.

'He is directing operations in the city, *sir*.'

'Whereabouts is he?'

'We don't know, sir.'

'You mean to tell me the Commissioner is not in touch with his office?'

The man looked blank.

'Do you know how the rioting started?' I asked.

'There was a fight between the Indian and Burmese dock labourers this morning and then the outside Burmans joined in.'

'How many people have been killed?'

'I don't know, sir.'

I was wasting precious time. I should never get a clear, statement till I found Mr. Merrikin or one of his European subordinates of the Imperial Police, and I left his office with that immediate intention. But the turmoil covered a wide area. As I made my way deeper into the city I perceived how difficult it would be to find him. Bands of Burmans passed me brandishing their swords; other bands were surrounding houses, from the upper windows of which Indians threw bricks. In some streets the mob was so thick that I could make no progress. For a long time I could detect no-one in authority. Neither side attempted to molest me or even turned their eyes towards me. It was like a nightmare; I had no idea what to do or whether I had any business to be there at all. I had never imagined such a situation—that, an officer empowered to arrest and punish, I should wander helplessly for hours in the midst of a riot.

It was nearly one o'clock when I found Mr. Merrikin. He appeared totally exhausted. With a body of police he was patrolling a side-street in an attempt to keep the Burmese from entering a row of Indian houses.

'Come a long with me,' I said, 'you must have a drink or you will collapse,' and took him in my car to the Silver Grill Restaurant in Fytche Square.

'What's happened? I'm completely in the dark.'

'We always thought the Burmans would turn on the Indians one day. Well, they've done it at last.'

'How did it start?'

'I don't know exactly, but some kind of a dispute arose in the docks between Indian and Burmese labourers. There was a fight and in no time the whole town was up, with armed Burmans pouring in from the suburbs in buses.'

'The situation's out of hand?'

'It is for the moment.'

'How many have been killed?'

'I don't know.'

A debate followed. I suggested that as many of us as possible should meet in his office and discuss the situation. Was it desperate enough to warrant calling out the troops?

Mr. Merrikin seemed dead beat. I could get no answer out of him. Failing to do more than fix a rendezvous at four o'clock in his office I left him in confabulation with his subordinates and hurried to my court, where I drew up a short report and submitted it to the Government. Sir Charles Innes and his advisers were at the hill station of Maymyo, twenty-four hours' journey away by train.

My report was hardly done when a man ran in to say that a number of terrified Indian labourers had taken refuge in the upper story of a wooden house next my court. Some Burmans had seen them enter and had surrounded the house, with the apparent intention of slaughtering them there. I hurried into the street, feeling more helpless than ever. Frowning and sinister, a band of Burmese roughs, armed with swords, were stalking on the pavement.

'What do you want?' I asked, going up to them.

'Those Indians inside have murdered Burmese women,' one of them answered me sullenly. 'A Burmese woman has had her breasts cut off. We cannot stand that.'

'I shall send for the police,' I replied, 'and have them taken into custody. If they have committed murder they shall be tried for it.'

I was surprised to see that the roughs were satisfied by my answer. 'Very well,' they said, 'we will wait.'

I went upstairs and telephoned urgently to the police office. The answer I received was that all the police were engaged in the city.

'You must send a few men somehow,' I urged. 'There are sixteen Indians in the house and they will all be killed.'

The sub-inspector at the other end promised to see what could be done.

I went out into the street again. The Burmans were treading round the wooden house like tigers.

'The police are coming shortly,' I said. 'You can leave it to me and go home.'

'We will wait,' they said.

In eighteen years I had never seen Burmans like that before. They had a suppressed ferocity which was very alarming.

I returned to my office, hoping the police would arrive soon. In a quarter of an hour a message was sent in by the leader of the Burmans to say that they could wait no more and proposed to deal with the Indians.

This was frightful intelligence. It had been humiliating enough to wander ineffectively in the wild streets, but was I now to be spectator of a massacre at my very door? There were a couple of Englishmen in an upper part of the building. We consulted together. Unfortunately, we were unarmed, as were our staffs. There was no hope of over-awing the Burmans outside.

I went out again to speak to them. 'The police have been delayed,' I said, 'there is so much going on in the town. But I guarantee that these Indians will be arrested and tried according to law.'

I looked at the Burmans. Some of them began crowding up a staircase at the top of which the Indians were hiding. The atmosphere was horrible; I could hardly breathe it, so charged it was with instant murder. The leader now approached me closely. He was a man of about thirty, his torso bare and muscular, a drawn sword in his hand.

'Your Honour will do well to step back into the court,' he said with extreme politeness.

I do not know whether I was in peril or not that moment, for one does not know what is in one's soul, and I do not know what I might have done. But I was spared the probing of that mystery, for a car drove up at full speed and from it disembarked a squad of police.

'Get the Indians down at once and march them off,' I said.

The police, who were Burmese, hustled their compatriots off the stairs and entered the upper rooms. The Indians were hiding where they could. They were in a state of extreme terror. I have never seen men accept arrest with greater pleasure.

'You will take them straight to the jail,' said the Burman leader.

'Be easy,' I said, 'they go straight to jail.'

At the thought of the protecting walls of the jail an expression of beatitude spread over the faces of the Indians. They were immigrants from Madras, who had come over to plough and plant the rice fields of the delta, afterwards to return home with a few rupees. Ignorant and timid, they had been hunted through the streets. Whatever other Indians might have done, they were wholly innocent. Rumour had fastened suspicion upon them. I think we were lucky to save their lives.

3. THE COLLOQUY ON THE ROAD

At half-past three I left the office and began driving through the streets to my rendezvous with Mr. Merrikin. There was no fighting in progress in the main thoroughfares, though traffic was suspended and crowds of people were watching from the pavements and from windows. As I went down Fraser Street in this lull I saw a familiar figure walking in the crowd. It was Mr. Booth Gravely, the Commissioner of the Pegu Division. At the moment he was the senior officer in Rangoon, as the Governor and his advisers were away.

I stopped at once.

'Where's Merrikin?' he asked. 'I've been trying to find him all day.'

I explained what I knew and he got into my car. We drove on to Dalhousie Street.

Entering Mr. Merrikin's room we found him in earnest consultation with his staff. A discussion ensued and certain points were cleared up. It seemed that the fight at the docks, which had started the conflagration had followed an action on the part of a British firm of stevedores, which ordinarily employed hundreds of Indian labourers to stow and unload cargo in the port. There had been an Indian strike and the firm had taken on Burmese labour to break it. (As a rule Burmans were not employed by stevedores, as they were disinclined for that kind of work.) The strike had been settled the previous evening and that morning, when the Burmans arrived to work, they were told that their services were no longer required. A number of Burmese women were there with their husbands' breakfasts in baskets. All of them had walked in a long distance. The sudden news that they were not wanted was an irritation. They felt that they had been made a convenience of by the stevedores. Having broken the strike, they could now clear out.

At this touchy juncture the Indians committed the grave indiscretion of laughing at the Burmese in front of their women. As the Burmese regarded the Indians as little better than rats, which had swarmed into the country to the detriment of the working classes of the native population, they were disinclined to tolerate any hilarity at a moment when they found themselves in a humiliating position. A preliminary blow or two was struck, which the Indians were foolish enough to return, with the result that within half an hour at least two hundred Indians were cut down or flung into the river. The news was through the city in a flash. Some Indian reprisals were probably taken at this point, and the story of the mutilation of a Burmese woman was carried into the suburbs. Hundreds of Burmans then hurried to town. There developed a civil commotion on a grand scale, which threatened to spread to the villages, and lead to the death of the numerous Indians scattered over the country.

As we sat round Mr. Merrikin's table we did not know all these facts; we had no idea, for instance, that as many as two hundred Indians had been killed; but we realized that the Burmese were in a wild mood, that they had already paralysed all public activity in the city, and that if west Rangoon, where they chiefly resided, were to move in organized force upon central Rangoon, where the Indians lived, there would be a very bloody fight and massacre. But Mr. Merrikin, as dogged a man as I have ever met, thought that he could regain control of the city without military help. If he had been caught unawares by an unprecedented situation, to meet which no plans had been made in advance, he was going to show that he could catch up and restore order with his own men. He had a deep regard for the Burmese; their behaviour that day appeared to him no worse than the ebullience of spoiled children; and he did hot care for Indians.

The first point was to get the law right, and I was asked to sign an order under Section 144 of the Criminal Procedure Code empowering the police to fire upon any assembly of five or more persons who might refuse to lay down their arms when ordered to do so. I did this at once, expressing the hope that the police would make full use of it, for the situation was decidedly more serious than Mr. Merrikin cared to admit. To call out the troops there and then seemed to me the right thing to do, but the rest were not disposed to agree when I suggested it.

At this moment Mr. Phipps, the Superintendent of the Port Police, arrived in a flurry. After saluting his chief he said: 'I have just received information, sir, that about a thousand Burmans armed with swords and iron bars are advancing in a body from the direction of the Botataung Pagoda towards the Indian part of the town.'

The Botataung Pagoda is on the river-front, eastwards, and an attack from that quarter was totally unexpected, as the Burmese centre was in the opposite direction.

The news threw us all into some confusion. It was imperative to stop the Burmans before they reached the inner streets, but we did not appear to have the necessary force. The bulk of the police were patrolling on the other side of the town. However, Mr. Merrikin was able to lay his hand on a dozen English sergeants of the Mogul Guard. With these we bundled into cars which were waiting at the kerb and set out for the region of the Botataung Pagoda. It had not occurred to me during the day to fetch my automatic from the house and I observed that Mr. Booth Gravely was similarly unarmed. The foolhardiness of starting on such an adventure without a weapon was not as clear to me then as it is now. The predicament in which I had found myself an hour earlier at the court had not taught me prudence. But none of us realized the full gravity of the situation.

In the party was my friend, Frank Fearnley-Whitting-stall, the Deputy Commissioner of Police. He was one of the best-known men in Burma at the time, having been Private Secretary under the previous régime. There was no cooler, more resolute officer in the country. Some years before he had won the King's Police Medal by an act of very conspicuous gallantry.

We stopped the cars at the corner of Eden Street and the main road to the Botataung Pagoda. Some distance down the road could be seen a large force of Burmans, whether a thousand or less it was difficult to say, swarming towards us as they flourished swords, bludgeons, and crowbars.

Mr. Merrikin strung his dozen sergeants across the road. They drew their revolvers and pointed them at the mob. I was standing behind the sergeants with Mr. Booth Gravely. He drew me aside a moment, and lifting up the carpet of his car showed me two very fine crowbars.

'Thanks,' I said, 'if necessary I know where to come.'

I remember this of Mr. Booth Gravely with pleasure. He strongly disapproved of the manner in which I had tried the Sen Gupta case, but he offered me a crowbar at a critical juncture.

We covered the crowbars again and returned to the sergeants. For some reason neither of us wished to be seen with a crowbar until it was unavoidable. I think we felt it might advertise our nervousness. For my part, I have never been in a more precarious position. I had just signed an order authorizing the police to fire on any five persons who refused to put down their arms. Within pistol shot were five hundred armed persons at the very least. But if we provoked them by a volley from our miserable force it was touch and go whether they would rush us. If they did, we had no chance; we should be hacked to pieces. If we withheld our fire, and they insisted on passing, many an Indian would be hacked to pieces that night.

The mob advanced, shouting and waving their weapons, till the foremost was not six feet from the sergeants. It was a moment of great anxiety. If the sergeants fire, we're done for, they're on top of us, I said to myself, and was on the point of getting the crowbar, when I noticed the faces of the Burmans. They were smiling. Fearnley-Whittingstall had also noticed this and, before any of us could take in the situation, had stepped in front of the sergeants and was arguing with the leaders.

'*Ma-maik-né!* You've got to go home and leave your weapons with me.' He wrested away two or three swords in a pleasant manner. The owners hardly liked to resist such a grand gentleman.

All this occupied barely a minute, but it completely changed everything. It seemed the most natural thing in the world for the rest of us to join Fearnley-Whitting-stall and copy his method. We walked with confidence into the middle of the insurgents, and speaking to them in their own language, and as if they were our sons, told them not to be bloody fools, and to get off home.

'But', said a youth to me with tears in his eyes, as I removed his iron bludgeon, 'I know for certain that a girl has had her breasts cut off by the Indians. Please let me go on.'

'My dear fellow,' I said, 'take it from me, it's not true. Anyhow, we'll see to it.'

'I didn't think', said another, 'that there was any objection to killing Indians. The Government is against them.'

'What d'you mean?'

'The police let them have it at your Honour's court not long ago.'

'But they attacked the police first.'

'They attacked us first to-day.'

'Well,' I said, 'you can't kill Indians. Get away home now or the Commissioner of Police will be angry with you.'

They went, but it was a close-run thing. Had we not realized in time that, despite their bellicose appearance, the Burmans' quarrel that day was only with the Indians, that, indeed, they believed us to be on their side, we might have been foolish enough to fire. A volley, of course, might have frightened them; but, if it had infuriated them, they were so close upon us that we could not have fired a second time. Fearnley-Whittingstall's instant grasp of the truth probably saved a number of lives.

I look Back upon this colloquy with the Burmans on the road to Botataung as one of the strangest moments in my life. Merrikin, Booth Gravely, Fearnley-Whittingstali, myself, the Burmans, the Indians—we were all characters in a drama which was not yet played out. Stresses, tensions bound us together, drove us apart, in accordance with the structure of the drama in which we were involved.

4. THE REFUGEES

That night, with the Indians all locked in their houses, the town was tolerably quiet, but at dawn the Burmese were on the move again and Mr. Merrikin found that without the assistance of the military he could not prevent them killing more Indians. There were too many of them, they were everywhere; all the Indian houses could not be guarded; nor could he resist an advance in force on the Indian quarter.

The British regiment stationed in Rangoon at that time was the Cameron Highlanders, one of the smartest regiments of the British Army. Its officers were mostly of good family and had private means and in these two particulars differed from the generality of the English in Rangoon. By noon on the 27th a detachment of the regiment occupied the centre of the Indian quarter, planting their machine-guns in Fraser Street in such a way as to make it impossible for the Burmans to invade the area.

Before the Camerons arrived I had been from an early hour about the town, watching the situation. Not that there was anything I could do, except inform myself. Mr.

Merrikin was making his own arrangements, blocking the roads into Rangoon to prevent further bands of roughs entering the city, and struggling by means of special constables to extend his grip down the narrow side-streets. I wandered in a rather futile way from place to place. At the corner of Fraser Street and Soolay Pagoda Road I found the special constables—English and Eurasians—without arms in the face of a mob of Indians who appeared to be on the point of taking reprisals. I got them revolvers from a gun-shop in the neighbourhood and went on to see where else I could be of use. Necessarily out of touch with what Mr. Merrikin was doing, I drifted later on into a ridiculous position, for when the police fired a volley, as they did about nine o'clock, some of their bullets passed over the bonnet of my car.

This contretemps convinced me that I was merely in the way. There was nobody to give me orders, nor could I give orders to anybody. Mr. Booth Gravely was in the same position. For the moment there was nothing to be done but to let the police get on with their work.

But this feeling of ineptitude passed quickly, for next morning Sir Charles Innes arrived in Rangoon from Maymyo. He went to the Mogul Guard, which had been made into a General Headquarters, and acquainted himself at first hand with the situation. By that time a state of armed peace had been established; the Burmans no longer roamed the streets in murderous bands. But the entire Indian population was barricaded in their houses, and, as most of the food shops belonged to them, provisions were becoming scarce. More important still, there was no conservancy, for that department was wholly manned by Indians. The paralysis of the conservancy meant that night-soil was not being removed. Despite trams and electricity, cinemas, and a university, Rangoon was entirely dependent upon Indians for the removal by hand of what in our cities is carried by water. To prevent both an epidemic and a scarcity of provisions it was essential to get the Indians out of their houses. But their nerve was shaken and they had no intention at the moment of exposing themselves to further massacre to oblige the general population. It was useless to tell them that the military and police concentrations now ensured their safety.

On the morning of his arrival Sir Charles sent for me. I had not seen him since the Sen Gupta trial, and came into his presence prepared to find his manner altered. This, however, was not the case.

'Collis,' said he, with his usual urbanity, 'I want you to take charge of the Indians who have been lodged for safety in the old lunatic asylum. Get them out and to work again as soon as you can.'

Thousands of the poorer Indians had deserted their homes, which in some cases had been destroyed by the Burmans, and had been allowed to take refuge behind the walls of what, until a year or two previously, had been the Rangoon Lunatic Asylum.

'Get them to work,' repeated Sir Charles. 'Tell them I guarantee their safety.'

'May I also tell them', I asked, 'that they can hope for some compensation, where they have been injured or their property destroyed?'

'I shouldn't say anything about that, I think,' he replied cautiously.

I went to the asylum at once. It presented an extra-ordinary sight. Into buildings and a space meant to accommodate about five hundred lunatics were crowded seven thousand Indian labourers of the kind who came over yearly from Madras to plough and reap the vast areas of the delta. Many of them were in bandages; they all appeared miserable and brow-beaten.

I was met by Mr. Tyabji and some young men in the white costume of Congress supporters. Their manner was a little cool, and no wonder. All the leaders they venerated in India were in prison and now the authorities in Burma had failed to protect the lives of Indians from a Burmese mob, and a mob which seemed to think it could murder Indians with impunity. With such ideas irritating them, the white-capped Congress youths regarded me frigidly. Moreover, they had been distributing free food to the refugees and felt an added virtue in doing what they considered the Government should have done.

'His Excellency is very anxious', I said, 'to see these people at work again.'

'When His Excellency can protect us and when we receive a promise of compensation, it will be time enough,' said Mr. Tyabji, on behalf of the refugees.

I saw at once that the Congress Party proposed to take advantage of the situation. If they could prevent the Indians from returning to work the inconvenience of no shops and no conservancy might enable them to bargain with effect. It was obvious that I should get no help from them. Nor was it possible to appeal directly to the labourers. I tried this with an interpreter, but the blank expression which met my statement that the Governor guaranteed their safety showed me that not one of my hearers believed a word of what I said. As far as I could see the refugees proposed to stay where they were, indefinitely.

At this impasse one of my staff whispered: 'Mr. Khan is the only man who can do it.'

Mr. Khan had arrived from India fifty years earlier with a blanket under his arm and cightpence in his pocket, but he happened to be a man of talent and so had no difficulty in becoming a millionaire. By 1930 he was the owner of large rice mills and a fleet of river boats. I may have done him some small service; at any rate he regarded me as a friend. So when I heard the whisper I said: 'Send for Mr. Khan.'

I forget where we met, but I remember the conversation well enough. It was conducted in Burmese.

'Your Honour has sent for me?' Mr. Khan was grizzled and tough, with remarkable eyes.

'His Excellency wants me to get the refugees out of the lunatic asylum, but they won't move. He proposes himself to visit the place to-morrow and daily afterwards. If I have to declare myself beaten he will have the advantage of me.'

Mr. Khan knew exactly what I meant. He saw all the implications, realized that he could do me a good turn, the Government, the public, and, he hoped, himself a good turn, and said: 'Your Honour can leave it to me. In five days' time there will not be one Indian in the asylum.'

I had not the slightest idea how he proposed to evacuate seven thousand Indians in five days, restore their confidence, square the Congress, find lodgings and food, employment and money; but I believed he could do it and I shook him by the hand.

Next day I visited the asylum in the course of the morning. Not a man had left so far, the crowd was as dense as ever. I had been told to expect Sir Charles at three o'clock. He attached the greatest importance to the evacuation. He had been using all his influence with the Indian members of the Legislative Council to get the shops open and work started, but with seven thousand labourers cowering in the asylum those who had their own irons in the fire were able to claim that the town was still unsafe.

He drove in at three o'clock to the minute. In spite of the emergency he observed some state and we all stood bareheaded.

'Well, Collis, you haven't been able to do much yet, I see,' he began, glancing at the miserable crowd.

'I am making my arrangements, sir,' I replied. 'In four days I ought to be able to clear the place.'

'I hope you're right.' He had a look round and left.

The next day when I went down I was told that Mr.
Khan had taken away a thousand men in the night. The
crowd certainly looked less dense, I thought. As there was
nothing for me to do in the asylum—Mr. Khan being the
magician and his sleight-of-hand beyond me—I decided
to inspect some of the damage which the Burmans had
done in the poorer Indian quarters of the town.

I particularly remember a line of labourers' tenements
in a narrow street off the docks. On the first day the Burmese mob had invaded the tenements, where many Indians
were taking refuge. It found its prey, I was told, perched
on the rafters out of reach. The Indians were ordered to get
down, and when they refused to moye the Burmans flung
their swords at them. The poor wretches fell to the
ground, where they were dispatched. The condition of the
tenements proved there had been savage play. The corpses
had been removed, but everything reeked of blood; boxes
had been broken open, their contents looted or slashed;
the very walls dripped blood; little pictures of the gods
had not escaped destruction.

The sight of this angered me. I knew well enough that
the upper-class Burmese had had nothing to do with the
massacre, that in many cases they had hidden Indian
fugitives with true Buddhist charity and at risk to themselves; I knew that they strongly disapproved of what the
mob had done; but I felt that their honour and reputation
demanded more than mere disapproval.

In this indignant frame of mind I met U Set, a Burman,
who was the official representative of the Government on
the corporation executive. 'You Burmans', I shouted at
him in a rage, 'want to impress the House of Commons
and get home rule! How are you going to explain this
massacre?'

U Set was not offended by my tone. He was distressed.

'You're just a pack of murderers,' I went on, getting
more heated. 'You slice up the Indians to-day; to-morrow

it will be the Chinese or the English. How are you going to get your own government?' I was fond of U Set.

'The thing has happened under an English government,' he complained.

That was a point, I had to admit. The massacre was, of course, an aspect of insurgent nationalism. The subservience of the Burmese in their own country had been, perhaps, the chief cause of it. The Government's ill-concealed opinion that they were not as fit as Indians to govern themselves and should get an inferior constitution had added vehemence to their onslaught. But I was too angry at the moment to listen to reason.

'If you are going to lay the massacre at the Government's door, well and good, there's nothing more to be said. But you're making a tactical error.'

In this way we wrangled all down the road. At last he said: 'Are the Indians leaving the asylum?'

'Some have,'. I admitted, 'but of course they want compensation. There's not only been murder, but looting too.'

'How many have been killed?'

'We shall never know. Perhaps three hundred, perhaps five.'

U Set was exceedingly depressed. 'Let's go and see the Governor and ask him about compensation.'

An appointment was arranged at Government House and we started. Two or three more had joined U Set, all leading Burmans.

When we were shown in Sir Charles was at his desk.

'These gentlemen want to raise the question of compensation.'

'Compensation is out of the question.'

We were shown out, but the Burmans were in good spirits. The move had whitewashed the whole Burmese nation, which had suddenly become more humane than the Government.

That night Mr. Khan evacuated another thousand by means known only to himself.

When I inspected the inmates of the asylum next morning the crush appeared definitely less. There were a mere five thousand in quarters planned for five hundred. One saw the ground here and there. But, seriously, could Mr. Khan clear the place within the time? He had only two more days if he were to keep his promise.

Sir Charles arrived in the afternoon. Somehow, I forgot to take off my hat. He glanced at it in surprise. I tore it off.

'You're not getting on very fast here,' he observed.

'There won't be a man in the asylum the day after to-morrow, sir,' I said rashly.

Sir Charles's gentlemanly expression did not alter. He looked round for five minutes, addressed a few words to the Indians through an interpreter, and departed. Later in the day he sent the Private Secretary to tell me that he was rather surprised at seeing so many Indians still there.

I had not met Mr. Khan since the first day and, my faith wavering for an instant, I now sent him a—message 'Can you do it in the time?'

'I can,' came the answer.

I had a game of golf. That night Mr. Khan moved three thousand. By myself I could not have induced one man to leave. When I saw it next morning the place looked empty. It had only four times as many people in it as it was meant to have. Sir Charles did not come down that day.

I was now sure Mr. Khan could do it. When I arrived about noon on the fifth day, I saw five men with bundles. They were on their way out. There was no one else. I rang up the Private Secretary. 'Please tell His Excellency that the asylum has been totally evacuated.'

I then wrote in and demanded a title for Mr. Khan. One was conferred on him in the next list.

CHAPTER SIX

1. AFTER THE MASSACRE

―――――――――――

Rangoon settled down quickly. No Burmans were sent up for trial except a couple who had had a desperate fight with the police. The hundreds of murders passed unpunished, because there was no evidence who had committed them. The massacre was called a riot, and an inquiry was opened, at which most of the witnesses were careful not to enlarge upon the atrocities committed by the Burmese. I was called, of course, and I believe my description of what I had seen in the tenement houses passed for a bold statement. The findings of the committee were directed chiefly to suggesting ways in which a repetition of what had happened could be prevented. The Indians got no compensation. In fact, it was difficult to compensate them; the bill would have been enormous, a just distribution of money very complicated. How could the families of those who had lost their lives have been relieved when the names or, indeed, the numbers of the dead were unknown, as were the addresses of their families in India? So they had to take it as all in the day's work. From time immemorial the Indian peasants have had the worst of it. With the resignation of their race they now tried to forget the frightful events of 26 May and of the following day or two, when they had been hunted round the town like vermin and their women ripped up, and went meekly about their work again, carrying burdens or slops, dragging rickshaws or handcarts, planting and ploughing, stowing or unloading cargo.

The Burmese proletariat walked with a lighter step.

They had shown the Indians their place. This was Burma, a land which had been independent for hundreds of years before it fell to the English. Too many Indians had crowded into it from their starving villages across the bay. They could live on nothing and undersell the Burmese, and there was a swarm of them too in the public services, particularly in the railways and the Prison Department. Well, they had been taught a lesson!

Short of violence to the Indians, these views were shared by the upper-class Bunnans, the clerks, the officials, the graduates, and the landowners. The time had arrived, they felt, when the problem of Indian immigration into Burma would have to be considered, and when Indians settled in Burma, from shopkeepers to barristers, would have to cease competing for power and money, and identify themselves with the common good of the native inhabitants. The Simon Commission Report would be published shortly. It would form a point of departure for the overdue consideration of all these matters.

A new superintendent of the Rangoon Jail selected this extremely inopportune moment to tighten discipline and punish breakers of it with severity. When it is said that he was an Indian and that the thousand-odd convicts in the jail were Burmese, what sort of tinder he was providing may be guessed.

2. THE MUTINY

Mr. Merrikin had come safely through the events described in the last chapter, but his health was giving way. He had already begun to complain of an irritation in the throat, a rawness at the base of it which was not alleviated by local treatment. Sir Charles also had been growing more and more unwell. The times were hard, he was working very long hours. If he had once hoped for a quiet five years as Governor he had been sadly disappointed, and was to be disappointed again.

Though calm had succeeded the events of May 1930 it was continually rumoured that other disasters were on the way. I have spoken of the gloomy prophecies in which the country people believed. Now it was said that 24 June would see a further upheaval. That was the day fixed for the publication of the Simon Commission Report. The rumour was so insistent that we all knew of it. What could be going to happen on 24 June? Mr. Merrikin and his colleagues were the last people to be unduly impressed by bazaar talk, but after the sudden outbreak of 26 May, which had taken him so much unawares, he was agitated by what he heard, and with the assistance of the C.I.D. tried to find out what sort of a ruction to expect this time. He could get no information. Would the Burmese turn on the Indians again or would the Indians, after brooding on their losses, suddenly rise and attack the Burmese? Not the slightest foundation could be found for either of these anticipations. Detectives inquired, searched, listened, but failed to unearth any plot. Yet the rumour remained as insistent as ever. There were no lack of informers. Everyone pointed to the other as the potential aggressor. But when accusations were examined they were found to have no substance. Everything except the rumour dissipated under scrutiny.

As the 24th approached anxiety increased. It was assumed that if a fresh upheaval occurred it would be connected with the Simon Report. On that assumption the most likely insurgents were the Indians, for Congress had condemned the Report in advance on the ground that its recommendations were bound to fall far short of dominion home rule. But Congress supporters in Rangoon were few and there was no sign that they were organizing labour for

a demonstration. Moreover, Congress policy was non-
violent, and the rumour spoke of a violent outbreak.

In the circumstances there were some officials who
dismissed the rumour as fantastic, but Mr. Merrikin was
not one of them. He had been in Burma for twenty years
and had had a vast experience up and down the country. He
knew that in the East a rumour, however unsubstantiated,
presages something, and he determined to take every
possible measure of precaution. He had been caught nap-
ping once; that was enough. On 24 June he would have out
the whole Civil Police on patrol and the whole Military
Police standing by in barracks with their ponies saddled.
He also suggested that the regular troops should march
in that day from Mingaladon, the cantonment twelve
miles away, but the suggestion was not adopted.

On the 24th I got up as usual about half-past six and
opened my newspaper. The main findings of the Simon
Commission were given in large print. One's eye ran on to
see what had been recommended for Burma. Separation—
yes, Burma was to be separated from India. I was profoundly glad, for I believed that Burma had a destiny of
her own and considered that the events of May had proved,
if the fact were ever in question, that the Burmese would
never submit to an Indian government with its Indian
policy for Burma. But what sort of a constitution had Sir
John recommended for Burma? It appeared that he had
made no recommendation beyond suggesting that something analogous to the constitution he had outlined for
India should be set up after further inquiry. The manner in
which he washed his hands of Burma was a little ominous,
I thought. It left in doubt what sort of a constitution Burma
would get after separation, a doubt which was bound to
arouse the fears of those who had agreed with Sen Gupta
when he said that, if Burma did not stand with Congress,
she would be obliged to accept an inferior constitution.
Everyone knew that the Burma Government had a sketch

for an inferior constitution up its sleeve. No doubt that would now see the air. I wondered vaguely how the Burmans in their then mood would take it.

Laying down the paper I looked out of the window and began thinking of the day which had just dawned and which was said to hold in its hours some surprising event. I was no longer living in Golden Valley in the house which faced towards the great pagoda. My room was on the upper story of a block of flats known as Prome Court and I could see, as I looked out, the Pegu Club, the centre of official gossip, while to my right over the railway bridge the turrets of the Rangoon Jail stuck up. The weather was very close. Heavy showers of ran fell daily, for the monsoon was a month old. That morning the sun was out, though immense banks of cloud were ranged on the southern horizon.

I left for court rather earlier than usual, because I felt I should be ready in the centre of the city, within easy call in case of emergency. I could not know that it would have been better to stay comfortably at home all day, that Prome Court was close to the spot where the unknown event which we all awaited was destined to happen.

At court I made inquiries. There was not the smallest sign of unrest in the town. Everyone, I was told, was going normally about his business. The shops were all open; the Indians were circulating freely. There was nothing to remark in the demeanour of the Burmese. The Chinese were smiling, hard at work as usual. Police, detectives, sergeants were poking about or standing to arms. They were all so strung up that a street vendor could hardly shout his wares without giving them a turn.

I had no cases of any interest. Till lunch I listened to some desultory evidence about counterfeit notes. By three o'clock I had finished my file. Having nothing more to do I rang up Fearnley-Whittingstall.

'We're playing golf, aren't we, at five, now that all's well?'
'Yes, old boy.'

'I suppose if anything was going to happen, it would have happened before this?'

'Nothing will happen now. The place is dead quiet.'

'Five o'clock, then, at Prome Road.'

'I'll be there.'

There seemed no point in hanging about, so I got into my car and drove home by a circuitous route, approaching Prome Court from the east. I had dawdled, looking idly here and there for any sign of trouble, but a slumbrous afternoon appeared to lie over the city. It was three-forty-five when I reached my rooms and ordered tea. While it was being brought I heard a sound of firing from the west. The butts used by the volunteers were in that direction and I supposed that they had started their afternoon practice. Tea arrived at once and I swallowed a cup. The firing continued, and deciding to make sure where the sound was coming from I asked my butler to go outside and ask.

He was back in a couple of minutes. 'They're shooting in the jail,' he said. 'There's a crowd on the road, looking.'

I then woke up. Something had happened after all—and in the jail, not in the town! I blamed myself for having wasted five minutes over tea, and, in the hurry forgetting to pick up my pistol, rushed down the stairs to my car. In a minute I was over the railway bridge and saw the north wall of the jail two hundred yards in front of me, behind which it was now certain a fusillade was taking place.

I was obliged to pull up because the road was blocked with cars. In one of them was the Finance Member of Council and his wife.

'What's happened?' I called.

'There's an outbreak of some sort in the jail.'

A policeman was holding up the traffic. I beckoned to him. 'I want to get through,' I said. 'I want to get round to the main gate on the south side.'

'No cars can pass this way,' he replied. 'The road ahead is unsafe, bullets are ricocheting down it.'

'Don't you know me? I'm the District Magistrate. Let me through at once.'

He was a stupid man and still tried to prevent me, but I pressed my car somehow through the block and steered past him and down the road at full speed. If there were any bullets I did not hear them, but I saw Military Police in a turret on the wall firing down into the jail. At the north-west corner I turned left and again left at the south-west corner, and was hammering at the main gate within three minutes.

A turnkey half opened the wicket and looked through. 'Let me in!' I ordered.

He drew back and I stepped into the porch, feeling I was late, yet apprehensive at the thought of plunging into a fight of which I knew nothing. There was no-one in the porch and I told the turnkey to open the inner wicket. He did so under protest, and I passed into the jail, which stretched away, an immense congeries of buildings, walls, compounds, gates, a maze of a place, in the middle of which some desperate fight was in progress, the reverbera-tions from which were now deafening, and from which bullets seemed to be flying at random.

I contemplated the scene with misgiving and regretted that from an imaginary sense of duty I had hurried away from my tea. It was a police and jail affair. There was nothing I could do, except look on, as I had looked on during the days of the massacre. But having come so far I could not go back. Moreover, it was my duty to assure myself that the authorities immediately concerned were on the spot. But how was I to arrive at the centre of the action?

At this moment I saw appearing round a corner Mr. Campbell, the Registrar of the University. What he was doing in such a place I could not guess. He came forward hurriedly.

'What's going on?' I said.

'A convict mutiny has broken out, and the Military

Police are massacring the convicts. I wish you'd tell them
to cease fire.'

'What d'you mean,' I said, 'massacring the convicts?'

'They're on the walls, firing volley after volley into the
convicts in the roundhouse.'

'Have the mutineers surrendered?'

'I don't know,' he said, 'but it's massacre, for the convicts are powerless.'

There was an irony in this alleged massacre, for the
Military Police were Indians and the convicts Burmese.

'Where's the centre of it all?' I said. 'Can you take me
there?'

He appeared to know the way, for he led on briskly
down winding passages between high walls, with sudden
corners. I felt alarmed. Bullets seemed to be flying over
our heads.

'Do you know where you're taking me to?' I said at
last. 'Don't lead me suddenly into a field of fire.'

'It's all right,' he assured me, 'they're not pointing this
way, I think.'

It seemed a long time before he halted me in front of a wall
higher than the rest, in the face of which was a small door.

'If you go through there,' said he, 'you will have arrived.'

With that he left me contemplating the door. I could
hear a tremendous noise, firing, shouts, but I could see
nothing, and to go through the door without knowing into
what I was stepping seemed to me the height of folly. For
all I knew the mutineers might be just behind it and I
should walk into them, or, what was equally possible, meet
a volley fired by the Military Police. As I stood hesitating
what to do the door was opened from the inside, and looking through I saw Fearnley-Whittingstall.

The sight gave me courage to enter and, trying to appear
less discomposed than was the case, I said to him lightly,
'I'm afraid our golf is off.'

To this attempted pleasantry he made no reply, for, as I

learned afterwards, I had arrived at the critical moment of the action.

In front of me, up an alley-way between two long workshops, I saw a roundhouse. Mr. Merrikin, whom I now observed, and Major Hare, the commander of the Military Police, told me, very laconically, that there were some four hundred convicts in the roundhouse, armed with guns they had taken from the prison guard, a desperate band who refused to surrender. Military Police were firing into the windows of the roundhouse from different angles. An occasional shot came from the convicts.

It was no time to ask questions, particularly as I could be of no assistance, and I stood quietly with the other officers, watching events. I now saw Colonel Flowerdew, the Inspector General of Prisons. He was wounded in the arm and very pale. Up till a few weeks earlier, when he was promoted, he had been superintendent of the jail and much liked by the convicts. I saw no sign of Major Bharucha, the new superintendent.

When Major Hare perceived that no further shots were coming from the roundhouse he concluded that the convicts' resistance was at an end and ordered his men to advance. We all followed them up the alley to the roundhouse. I saw them reach the windows, lean in and fire upon those inside, and then rush the door. It still looked to me as if we might be engaged in a hand to hand fight with a desperate remnant, and I was also apprehensive of attack by other convicts from the side buildings, as our flank was unprotected. But my fears were groundless. Major Hare at that instant gave the order to cease fire. There had been a general surrender. I confess that to me, at least, it was a great relief.

I glanced at my watch. It was 4.25 p.m., only half an hour since I had been sitting in my flat, drinking tea. I do not suppose that I can remember in such detail any other half-hour in my life.

The scene in and about the roundhouse was startling. Thirty-four convicts were dead or dying, sixty were wounded, some very grievously. The confined space seemed covered with corpses. Of the prison staff two were dead and eight were wounded. The .303 bullet at close range has a lacerating effect where it leaves the body, and I saw some convicts, still living, who had been shot through the back, with terrible gaping wounds on their breasts. Unaccustomed to battlefields, I thought they had been hit by buckshot in front, for the prison guard used buckshot, but I was wrong, for the wounds were caused by the emergence of high-velocity bullets. In the Western world one would not see such wounds, for clothes would cover the place, but in the East, where clothes are not well secured, they fall off in a fight. The scene was not the less grim, in that all the dead convicts were naked.

The police and prison staff were soon busy, some carrying off corpses by the hands and feet, some collecting the cowed mutineers into batches and marching them to the cells. Both convicts and warders were in a pitiable state of nerves. As one batch was taken past me the warder in charge waved his revolver through inability to keep his hand steady. Fearnley-Whittingstall turned on the man with a rending oath, which steadied him, as if two fears can balance each other. I saw one curious sight. A sergeant of the Mogul Guard—I think it was Gallagher, and he was a conspicuous figure, for he was covered from head to foot with blood, not his own but what had spurted on him during the encounter—this fellow rapped a convict with his baton on the back of the neck to encourage him to hurry on his way to the cells. The blow had an unexpected effect. Six golden sovereigns fell from the man's mouth. He had secreted them in a pouch under his tongue, a bank upon which he drew, I suppose, when he wished to buy concessions from the jail staff. Sovereigns had long been out of circulation, and to see six of them burst from a convict's mouth in that scene of carnage made me feel, suddenly, as if I were myself part of a surrealist picture.

Meanwhile Mr. Booth Gravely with the Finance Member of Council had arrived on the field. As the former passed me he raised his eyebrows and said: 'Another inquiry?'

3. THE INQUIRY

Booth Gravely was right. On 26 May, two days later, I received a letter from the Governor-in-Council directing me to hold an inquiry into the circumstances of the mutiny. Why had the convicts broken out? Was their object that of most convicts—to escape—or had they another or a further motive? And had the suppression of the mutiny been effected in a proper manner?

At the time of the receipt of the letter I was still in complete ignorance of the cause of the outbreak. On the 25th I had visited the jail and ascertained a few preliminary facts. Apparently the mutiny had begun at three o'clock, the very moment I was telephoning to Fearnley-Whittingstall about golf. It was confined to the western section of the jail, in which were the workshops. The door through which I had gone, with such trepidation was a door from the main jail into that section. Four hundred convicts out of a much larger jail population had been involved. They had seized during the first few minutes a gateway on the west wall, called the Rear Guard, and captured four rifles and thirty-five rounds of ammunition. In control of this exit, they did not try to escape. No-one could explain why they had not done so. At about 3.15 the Military Police, roused by the alarm sounded on the gongs of the main gate, which reached their ears as they stood by in their lines under the emergency instructions for the day, had mounted their ponies and in charge of their native officers galloped to the jail, which they immediately surrounded. Five climbed a turret and poured volleys into the mutineers. The telephone summoned the senior officers, who came up about 3.35 and entered the door in the wall about 3.45. During the quarter of an hour before I appeared they had brought the situation under control. That for half an hour the Military Police had had no English officer to limit their fire accounted for the heavy casualties.

Such was the outline of events. I knew little more than that outline when I received the Government's orders to hold the inquiry. Why the convicts did not rush out of the jail by the rear gate when they were in control of it seemed to me a mystery which, if explained, might disclose the cause of the mutiny.

On the afternoon of the 26th I went to the jail with the Government's instructions in my pocket, and asked the superintendent, Major Bharucha, his staff, and the convicts for their co-operation. While I did so I was impressed by the abject and furtive expression on the faces of the staff and by the sullen air of the convicts. I warned them all that the inquiry would open next day and returned to my office.

There I found a letter waiting for me. It was from a Burmese woman, one of the non-official visitors of the jail, and stated that if I called on the writer she could give me information of the first importance relative to the mutiny. I met her that same evening.

'Do you want to know the object of the mutineers?' she asked abruptly.

'Certainly,' I replied, 'but was it not to escape?'

'That was not their primary object,' she said earnestly. 'They desired first to kill Major Bharucha.'

'What proof of that can I get?'

'Ask the convicts.'

'But they will never confess to such a criminal design.'

'Yet there may be convicts who will admit that such a design existed.'

I took her point, thanked her, and departed.

Next morning I went to the main hospital, where thirty-three convicts were lying wounded. If any of them could be induced to speak about the cause of the mutiny it seemed to me that such a statement should carry much weight, for, cut off from the other convicts, they were unlikely to have conspired to tell an agreed story. I was taken to the two wards which they occupied and found them in bad case, suffering grievously from their wounds. Selecting a man in one of the rooms who seemed in less pain than his fellows, I entered into an informal conversation with him, at last asking him plainly why the convicts had mutinied. He hesitated to answer. He did not say, as he might have said without odium, that they had conspired to escape. To induce him to speak, I told him that I was not conducting a judicial inquiry, that he was not on oath, and that his name would not be made public. At that assurance he said cautiously that he had heard that the object of some of the convicts had been to kill Major Bharucha. 'Ma-kan-naing-bu—we couldn't bear it,' he added. I was unable to press him further, because he fell back exhausted on his pillow.

In the adjoining ward I examined another convict and got a similar statement.

On leaving the hospital I fitted what I had heard to the strange fact that none of the convicts had attempted to escape when they had had the chance, and came to the conclusion that a good deal of light had already been thrown on the mutiny. It remained for me to see whether the rest of the evidence would support or clash with what I had so far learned.

I began my investigations the next day and at the end of a week was able to put together the following sequence of events.

The afternoon of the 24th was cloudy and still, the temperature standing at about 88° F. Eleven hundred convicts, the great majority of whom were Burmese, were at their tasks in the workshop enclosure, hammering, chipping, weaving mats, or pounding rice, to all appearance resigned and wholly submissive to the Indian and Eurasian warders who directed them, as one more dull day of their sentences wore through. Five Indian sentries watched from the top of the Rear Guard. Each had a Martini-Henry rifle, a weapon popular during the last years of Queen Victoria's reign, with seven rounds of buckshot and three of blank. Near the workshops were a couple of motor-lorries connected with a jail press, which was worked partly by convicts and partly by a paid staff from outside.

At three o'clock one of the lorries prepared to leave. To do so it had to pass beneath the guard house through a passage, which on the prison side had a door made of iron bars and on the other a wooden door, which led into a courtyard in front of the western gate, a massive portal of wood studded with iron. A turnkey opened the door of iron bars and allowed the lorry to enter the passage under the guard. As the turnkey was about to enter the passage after the lorry a convict crept up behind him and struck him on the head with a piece of iron. Two other convicts snatched away his bunch of keys and assisted the first to batter him into insensibility. Quickly, then, they disabled the driver of the lorry, and with the keys locked the door between them and the main body of the convicts. The other keys fitted the outer door of the passage, the big gate, and a small door which led from the passage to the guard-room upstairs. The sentries heard the commotion under their feet, but they could see nothing, nor could they descend to the passage, because the door between them and it was locked.

Two jailors, who were patrolling the work-enclosure, catching sight of the wounded lorry-driver in the passage under the guard, now rushed up, and asked the sentry above their heads to throw them down a musket, with which they proposed to fire through the door. The sentry complied, but the stock of the musket was detached by its fall and the weapon became useless. A second rifle was then thrown down, but before the jailors could pick it up four hundred convicts, armed with tools, bludgeons, and crowbars, burst from the workshops towards the guard. The two jailors ran for their lives.

The sentries on the Rear Guard now began to beat the alarm gong, the sound of which was audible at the main gate in the south wall, but they were afraid to fire on the convicts, who, brandishing their weapons, stood immediately below them. It must be borne in mind that the guards and the whole staff of the jail were Indian or Eurasian, and that Indians had not been able to stand up to Burmans in the recent disturbances.

The three convicts under the guard house now unlocked the door between them and the rest, and forty mutineers entered the passage where the lorry stood, opened the door leading upstairs to the guard-room and scrambled up to attack the sentries. The sentries did not make a stand at the head of the stairs, nor fire down on the convicts as they came up in single file, but retreated along a gallery on to the top of the outer wall, from which they jumped to the ground outside the jail. They were wise not to stand; the convicts would have butchered them.

With the seizure of the Rear Guard there was nothing between the convicts and liberty. The two doors in the passage beneath the guard house were open and they had the key to the west gate. The senior staff in the Main Guard in the south wall were still not fully aware of what was happening, because the alarm gong on the Rear Guard had been stopped by the assault, when only a few strokes had been given.

But the convicts did not unlock the west gate and escape; they prepared themselves for a further struggle.

In the enclosure were six gallons of methylated spirits in tins. These were broached and the spirit served out. A hundred of the mutineers were soon fighting drunk. A proficient in magic was set to paint figures on the chest and arms of as many as possible to render them invulnerable. The two lorries were driven into the yard between the Rear Guard and the west gate, where they remained ticking over and ready to carry the prisoners comfortably into the town as soon as the word was given. But there was a task still to be accomplished, and the nature of it was indicated by loud cries of 'Where is the superintendent?' It was anticipated that he would shortly arrive to cope with the mutiny, when they could seize and do him to death. The seven hundred convicts who had not joined the mutineers crouched where they could, hiding those of their warders of whom they were fond. Other warders concealed themselves as they might, a disused boiler being found very useful.

Meanwhile the staff in the Main Guard had awoken fully to the situation. The alarm gongs were sounded to summon the Military Police, who surrounded the jail in record time. The superintendent, called by a telephone message, arrived from his house, and, since he was a prudent man and guessed the intentions of his charges, declined to expose himself to their animosity. The best course was to let the police reduce them, while he stationed himself in the Main Guard.

Having postponed their escape in order to deal with the superintendent, the mutineers were now in a quandary. It was still open to them to sally in force from the west gate and engage the police, afterwards scattering into the town, but they were not disposed to abandon their first design, even though five sepoys had climbed into a turret on the north wall and were beginning to pick them off. To get at the superintendent, however, was the difficulty. At this point a number of them made an attempt to enter the main jail, in order to find him wherever he might be, but a heavy fire was directed upon them as they sought to break in the wicket gate in the dividing wall. They were obliged to fall back.

At this stage of the battle the police carried the Rear Guard by assault from outside and from it poured volleys into the mutineers, whose way of escape was thus blocked. But the mutineers were by no means cowed and took up a position in the roundhouse, upon which the fourteen work-shops converged, resolved on a fight to the death. If they could not escape they still hoped to kill the superintendent.

So far the battle had been between Burmese prisoners and Indian police, for no Europeans had yet arrived, but it was now after half-past three, and first Mr. Merrikin with Mr. Fearnley-Whittingstall and a squad of the Mogul Guard, and then Major Hare and Colonel Flowerdew, appeared at the main gate. They inquired for the superin-tendent, and were shown upstairs to the rooms above the main gate, where they found him directing from the top floor a heavy fire of buckshot towards the work-enclosure, though the distance exceeded the effective range of his shot.

Noise and smoke are much used in battles, but Mr. Merrikin, who had his English prejudices, was not im-pressed by these stage effects, and without cordiality desired to be informed of the seat of the disturbance. The superintendent received this request with com-plaisance; like everyone else he admired the police.

'The disturbance', he said, waving his hand, 'is over there and I shall tell a reliable man to show you the way to it.'

Guided by a convict, Mr. Merrikin and his staff entered the main jail. Common prudence suggested that, before he ventured into the workshop enclosure, he should make a reconnaissance. His guide, who was no other than Pollard, the fifty-thousand-cigarette man, to the state of whose hands Sen Gupta had directed my attention, took him into an upper dormitory near the enclosure wall. But the window was not high enough to command a view of what was happening beyond.

Mr. Merrikin descended and consulted his colleagues. There was no doubt that a pitched battle was in progress between the Military Police under their native officers and the convicts under their leaders, and clearly it was his duty to assume command of the police and terminate the mutiny. But how was he to do so, how was he to enter the field and get control? The quickest, and the most dangerous, course was to go into the enclosure by a door without further reconnaissance, and on this he decided. The party advanced towards the wicket gate which I have already described, guided by Pollard and supported by the sergeants of the guard, Sullivan, Winder, Gallagher, and the redoubtable Ryan.

Mr. Merrikin was stricken, as was I later, with doubt when he saw the wicket. To open it and go in was a leap in the dark. The noise behind it was highly disconcerting, because the Military Police a few minutes earlier had taken the Rear Guard and from that elevation were in fact pouring shot in the direction of the door. However, there was nothing for it; he had to go in, unless he desired to follow the example of the superintendent and allow the combatants to fight out the issue by themselves, a course against which, as I have said, he was prejudiced by his English notions. At the moment when he thus decided to risk his life he was a dying man, though he did not know it, for a huge cancer was consuming his vitals. His face was grey and drawn; but with a jaunty air he signed to Pollard to open the door, and marched in, followed by the others.

The first few minutes were confusion, while bullets and ricochets screamed or spattered the wall. But the mutineers in the roundhouse did not attempt a sally; had they done so it is difficult to see how the police party could have saved themselves except by instant retreat. Soon, however, the sepoys caught sight of the officers and ceased fire. Major Hare got into touch with them, brought fifteen men down from the Rear Guard on to the ground, and, dividing them into three parties, ordered them to re-open fire from three angles on the roundhouse, sighting up the alleys between the workshops, in which the convicts who had not joined the mutiny were lying in terror.

Some of the mutineers in the roundhouse now found they had had enough—they were those who were sober—and made signs of surrender. Major Hare ceased fire and shouted to them to come out, but they were afraid to do so. Accordingly Colonel Flowerdew volunteered to walk up the alley-way and parley with them, counting on the fact that they knew and liked him. In this perilous course he was supported by Major Hare, and the two of them advanced, calling on the convicts to lay down their arms. When they were within fifteen yards of the roundhouse one of the more desperate mutineers fired a charge of buckshot, wounding the colonel in the arm. He fell, but was helped back to safety by a convict called Reynaud, a Eurasian, who ran to his assistance.

This episode suggested that the mutineers were still uncowed and as dangerous as ever. Fire was reopened upon them with intensity. It was at this moment that I entered the enclosure.

The fire had its effect and surrenders began. Many convicts, some of them wounded, rushed from the round-house and threw down their arms. They were collected in batches and sent into the main jail. When it was felt that the psychological moment had arrived for a frontal attack upon the remaining desperadoes word was passed, and, as I have described, we stormed the roundhouse. But there was no hand to hand fight, because the sepoys were able to shoot down at close range those who still resisted. Major Hare gave the cease fire as soon as it was clear that the rest had submitted.

Such was the narrative of events disclosed by my inquiries. It showed a desperate mutiny, the significance of which was interwoven with current history. The mutineers had chosen the 24th of June for their attempt because they also had heard the rumour that a disturbance was expected that day outside. But it was a fatal choice for them, because, as no other disturbance occurred, the expectant forces of the law were the more ready to pounce on them. Yet, for all that is known, the rumour referred to the mutiny itself. So crookedly do events unfold themselves and so delphic may be a true anticipation.

As for their intention to kill the superintendent, the Burmans outside the jail had been slaughtering Indians, and the Burmans inside it were in no mood to submit to an Indian who, they considered, was not treating them with the humanity which they had received from his English predecessor in office. At another time the superintendent's measures might not have caused a mutiny, but a tightening of discipline at that particular moment by an Indian was a dangerous course. If the police forces had been engaged elsewhere that day the convicts would have seized the whole jail and caught their man. When they had dealt with him they would have left in a body and, as their leaders were murderers and men who were serving long terms for crimes of violence, it is unlikely that, drunk with blood and methylated spirits, they would have dispersed quietly. The Indians in the town would have had another wild night and many would not have seen the dawn of the 25th. As it turned out, the Burmans were the sufferers; they only succeeded in killing two of their opponents and wounding eight. But the episode was not merely the worst mutiny which had ever happened in a Burma prison; it was deeply symptomatic of the disturbed condition of the country.

CHAPTER SEVEN

1. SIR CHARLES GOES ON LEAVE

In July Mr. Merrikin felt much worse, and one day, when his forces seemed very low, he went to a doctor. An examination was made and the dreadful truth revealed. Sentenced to death, he decided to meet it in his own country, and, after handing over his appointment to Fearnley-Whittingstall, sailed for Europe. As this story shows, he was a man of not more than average perceptions. But he knew how to stand up without fuss to an armed mob and he knew how to die. Those are qualities.

On 12 August Sir Charles Innes left for England on four months' sick leave. I went down to the wharf to see him off and remember the good-natured handshake which he gave me when I hurried up, rather late. His luck had been out; he was now seriously ill; but at the prospect of getting home he seemed quite animated. He had, of course, no inkling that during his absence an event more startling than the earthquake, the massacre, or the mutiny would take place.

He had handed over the governorship to Sir Joseph Maung Gyi, a Burman. This acting governorship was the highest official honour a Burman had ever received under English rule. Sir Joseph had been educated in Burma, had been called to the English Bar, and had held appointments in Siam, later becoming a judge of the High Court at Rangoon, and then Home Member of Council. He was an experienced man, but as Acting Governor his position was difficult. The Burmese as a whole refused him their confidence, though they were flattered by the appointment of one of their own nation to high office. He depended entirely upon the countenance of the three or four officials who held the top appointments in Rangoon. Mr. Lloyd, who had taken his place as Home Member, Mr. Booth Gravely, the Commissioner of Pegu, and Mr. Leach, who became Chief Secretary at this time, were men against whose wishes he could go only by seeking support in Delhi or London, and he had not the slightest intention of allowing any difference with them to reach a point where he would have to seek that support. His decisions in Council would follow the majority and his decisions out of council would be well founded on official advice. This attitude was admirably suited to carry him successfully through his four months as Acting Governor, provided that routine was undisturbed by untoward events. The peculiar character of his position may be better understood if I add that he was not a member of any of the three English clubs, nor could he, even as Acting Governor, have sought election with any confidence. But if the members of the clubs did not accept him as a social equal, they were ready to pay him due respect in his official capacity as long as he proved his sense and *bona fides* by following the advice of his English subordinates. For Sir Joseph to have made a stand over a matter because he believed that he was right would, in such conditions have been like going into a battle which one was bound to lose. No-one but heroes or madmen go into such battles, and Sir Joseph was a sane man who admired heroes from the proper distance. I knew him well, and he had my regard; there was a mellowness in his address, he had a charming humanity. That it was his lot to be so hedged in prevented him from always appearing the dignified and sympathetic person which he really was.

When he took over his duties the atmosphere in Burma was highly charged. Never since the fall of Mandalay had the Burmese spirit been so alive. While the politicians were hoping for a conference in London from which they might bring back a free constitution, the peasantry, whose state of mind had been disclosed in their set against the Indians, were dreaming of more violence, this time against the English. Both politicians and people were profoundly dissatisfied. The former believed that the Government of Burma would do all it could to prevent them from getting a fair deal in London, that it would come between them and Parliament as they held it had come between them and Sir John Simon, and would represent them, confidentially and by innuendo, as being less fit than Indians for home rule. In support of this belief they pointed to the constitution for Burma which the Government was drawing up. Sir Charles had placed a Mr. Lister on special duty to draft it, and it was no secret that if his draft were accepted Burma would become something like a Crown colony. That their own Governor should not stand up for them with his superiors in London, that the head of Burma should belittle the Burmese and make the task of proving their worth more difficult, seemed to the leaders an act of perfidy. They did not believe that he was really ill and conceived that the object of his journey to London was to get in first with his views, before the delegates arrived, and spoil their chance of impressing Parliament with their case. Sir Charles, of course, can have had no intentions of the kind; and in any case his influence in London was far less than the Burmese supposed. For them a governor loomed a tremendous figure and it was impossible that they should realize what a metamorphosis he underwent the moment he stepped out of Victoria Station.

The distrust felt by the politicians communicated itself to the village people, and hardened their resolution to take a desperate course.

This unrest did not wholly escape the English residents, who reacted to it by becoming more rigid on their side, less inclined to concede an inch of prestige and more ready to deny that the *status quo* could be changed.

It goes without saying that the administration of the law should take no account of a particular situation in a country; it should march on oblivious of political or social exigencies. In easy times this detachment is taken as a matter of course, but the year 1930 in Burma was no easy time, and an impartial administration of the law was not taken as a matter of course. I am about to describe an ordinary motor case of the sort which comes before the English courts every week and is hardly given the notice of a paragraph, and I shall show that, because it raised fundamental questions, at that time much in debate, a detached application to it of the law caused extraordinary excitement.

2. THE LIEUTENANT OF THE CAMERONS

At about twenty minutes to nine on the night of 28 August a motor accident occurred in the centre of the garden city where the Prome road crosses Halpin Road, close to the Pegu and Gymkhana Clubs. It was from the Gymkhana Club that the motorist responsible for the accident had just come. He was a young lieutenant of the Cameron Highlanders, Fortescue[1] by name, and from seven o'clock onwards he had been talking with his friends at the club bar and partaking of those refreshments which are consumed in Burma on a hot night. At half-past eight or so he looked at the clock and saw he would be late for mess, for he had to get to Mingaladon, twelve miles out of the town, where his regiment was quartered. Saying good night to his friends he hastened to the place where his car was parked and drove out of the club premises into Halpin Road. From the gate of the club to the cross-roads was a

---

[1] This was not his real name: see preface.

distance of a third of a mile, the road being straight and broad, and he drove down it at a smart pace, passing two cars on the way. It was a fine night.

At the cross-roads a traffic constable was on point duty. He stood on a wooden platform, and to control the traffic manipulated a green and red light. The cross-roads were the most dangerous in the garden city, for the Prome Road was the main road out of Rangoon to the north, while Halpin Road carried the evening traffic to and from the Gymkhana Club. For that reason the Commissioner of Police had posted there at that hour of the day the most experienced traffic constable in the force, an Indian from the Punjab, called Dawood Khan.

When Mr. Fortescue was still some distance from the cross-roads Dawood Khan gave the green light to a cyclist and a car on the main road, thereby blocking Mr. Fortescue with the red light. That officer, however, did not slacken his speed. He continued on his course against the red light and collided with the car on the main road to which the constable had given right of way.

That car was going at some twelve miles an hour. In the back seat were three persons, a Sino-Burman called Ah Khee, who was an assistant in a European firm, and his aunt and cousin, a girl of about eighteen. The point of impact was where the girl was seated. The collision was so violent that the Burman's car was sent sixty feet across the road, in the course of its career spilling the three occupants of the back seat. When it came to rest it had turned completely round and was without one of its back wheels.

Dawood Khan immediately jumped down from his platform, the cyclist dismounted, and various people came running from the adjacent houses, for the crash had been loud. They found Mr. Fortescue unhurt, though his car was stove in at the radiator, but the Burmese party was not so lucky. In a semi-conscious condition the two women were taken to hospital, where it was disclosed that the elder woman had a fractured skull, while the girl's pelvis was broken and her bladder ruptured.

The accident was reported at once to the traffic department, and next day an inspector went to Mingaladon cantonment and there arrested Mr. Fortescue. At the police station he was charged under Section 338 of the Indian Penal Code with grievously hurting two Burmese women by rashly and negligently driving his car over a cross-roads against a red light, an offence punishable with a maximum of two years' imprisonment or a fine of seventy-five pounds, or with both. The case was not under a traffic Act, but was a regular criminal prosecution, such as might be taken against a man who fired a gun at a cat crossing a crowded street and wounded a pedestrian.

The police charge came to me in the usual way. I had the discretion either to try the case myself or transfer it to any of my subordinate magistrates, but as the accused was an Englishman I adopted the procedure generally followed in such circumstances and entered the case on my own file, fixing 11 September for the first hearing.

So far there was nothing to show that a situation was developing. The action taken by the police could not have been more correct. Mr. Fortescue, though an army officer and a member of a crack regiment, had been arrested and charged as if he had been any person subject to the law. But it was hardly thought that he would be tried without special consideration. That was the general assumption. When it was realized by the regiment, however, that I was trying the case, some uneasiness was felt and it was recalled that in the Hughes trial nine months before I had steered a somewhat independent course. The same sort of thing might happen again. If this was disquieting, the facts of the case itself were not less so. To drive at speed through traffic lights as well-known as those on Halpin Road, and to run into another car with such force as nearly to kill its occupants, raised the question of sobriety, since a magistrate would be unlikely to take the view that an educated man in full command of his faculties might do this. Indeed, a moderate insobriety would be the kindest explanation, for to suppose its absence would suggest deliberate contempt for the law and the safety of the public. Doubly agitated by these reflections and by what they knew of me, Mr. Fortescue's brother officers decided to spare no expense and to engage Mr. McDonnell, the lawyer who had defended Hughes. Not only had Mr. McDonnell the reputation of a successful advocate, but he was also *person a grata* with some of the senior officials. His fee was high, very high, but the mess fund could find it. Everything possible must be done to avoid a sentence of imprisonment, which on the plain facts might well be imposed. For one of their officers to go to jail in a place like Rangoon was unthinkable.

I myself, busy with my routine work, gave the case little thought during the fortnight between the date of the accident and of the first hearing, though I knew it would be an unpleasant case, for I had read the police papers. During my time at Rangoon I had already tried some three or four Europeans for running over Indian or Burman pedestrians, on each occasion being able to acquit them of criminal negligence, either because it was the pedestrian's fault or for lack of evidence. The Fortescue case, however, was going to be different. I had never yet been obliged in a trial of any kind to sentence an Englishman to imprisonment, but I knew well enough that if I had to do so on this occasion there would be an outcry. What I did not anticipate was the loudness of the outcry.

3. THE SENTENCE OF IMPRISONMENT

The case was called on 11 September. The Crown was represented by the Assistant Public Prosecutor, U Myint Thein, a young Burman of mild and gentlemanly demeanour. Mr. McDonnell, for the accused, had a junior at his elbow. Police evidence was first taken, the traffic constable explaining how he gave Mr. Fortescue the red light before the cyclist and the car containing the Burmese ladies began to move over the cross-roads. This implied that the accused while still a distance down the road had the light against him, because the other car was crawling along. Medical evidence was recorded, the damage to the two cars and their position after the accident was noted, and four eye-witnesses were examined, their statements supporting the constable in every particular.

An adjournment was then given till 19 September, as the police wished to call the elder of the two injured women, for it was anticipated that by then her fracture of the skull would be sufficiently healed to permit of her giving evidence. Accordingly, on that day, her head in bandages and looking very feeble, she made her statement, without animosity and with perfect clarity. With her niece and nephew she was being driven slowly down the Prome Road by their chauffeur. When they were crossing Halpin Road after receiving the right of way there was a shout of warning, and she remembered nothing more till she woke in hospital.

The prosecution closed its case at this point. It had established that the accused had run through the lights and caused the accident, but, short of saying that he was on his way from the Gymkhana Club, left it to me to assume why he had done so.

Under the law of procedure I was entitled to call for any evidence which might be necessary for the full understanding of a case. In the Sen Gupta trial I had exercised that right in favour of the accused. The question was now whether I should direct the police to inquire how much Mr. Fortescue had drunk before leaving the bar of the Gymkhana Club. I shrank from that course, because I thought the evidence would tell heavily against him. It would have been better for me if I had been less sensitive on that score, a little suffer with the accused and his counsel. In the sequel it was never established by direct evidence what condition the accused was in when he left the club bar, but his actions immediately afterwards raised the presumption that he was probably muddled or made reckless by liquor. It would have been far more satisfactory had this presumption, however legitimate and inevitable it was, been transformed into a fact to which there was direct testimony, because while I was bound, if I wanted to make sense of the affair, to draw the presumption and assess the penalty accordingly, the fact that it was only a presumption enabled the supporters of the accused to say that there was no evidence to show that he was the worse for drink.

Mr. McDonnell, of course, perceived that some explanation of his client's disregard of the red light was necessary, and he evolved an ingenious theory. There were at that date only a few places in Rangoon where traffic lights were used and these were all manipulated by hand by the constable on duty. Some of these constables had been known on occasion to switch their lights without due consideration from red to green and back again, with the result that the driver of a car, as he approached a crossroads, would be given, perhaps on a wet night and a slippery road, the red light when he was too close to draw up. There was no intermediate yellow light. That was what had happened in his client's case, said Mr. McDonnell; he had been given the red light when he was on top of the cross-

roads. As this theory did not square with the presence on
the cross-roads of the other car, which in the circumstances
described by the prosecution, and because of the relative
speed of the two cars, would have had to enter the crossing
against the red light, it was a very poor defence. Moreover,
there was no evidence that the constable had done anything of the kind alleged.

When Mr. McDonnell perceived that this defence was
unlikely to stand scrutiny and that the presumption
against his client's sobriety was unshaken, he became
alarmed and tried to take the case out of my court. First,
he asked that the trial should be transferred to the High
Court Sessions, quoting a section of the law which allowed
such transfer in certain conditions where parties were of
different race and there was animosity. That would have
given Mr. Fortescue an English jury, and in Burma
English juries generally took a lenient view of crimes committed by Englishmen. I pointed out that the transfer was
impossible under the law, as the police, not the Burmans,
had brought the case. Moreover, there was no sign of
animosity, for the injured parties had made moderate
statements. Mr. McDonnell, though he had the right of
appeal against my order, accepted it as correct, but shortly
afterwards he made a second attempt to get his client out
of a dangerous position by asking me to allow the case to
be compounded. The police, he said, had no objection and
the injured women were willing to accept the substantial
compensation which his client was ready to disburse.

The law gave me discretion to allow composition. But,
clearly, to allow it at that late stage, when the accused's
conviction was certain, when allegations had been made
against the efficiency of the police and public policy
demanded an order by authority, would have been to
shirk responsibility. The case was by this time the sole
topic of conversation in the town. The military, their
friends among the officials, and their lady friends, had not

concealed their opinion of the prosecution. They talked at large in clubs and at dinner tables and abused the police up and down. In such an atmosphere to have granted composition would have been to bow to clamour. I therefore refused to grant it.

These two applications by Mr. McDonnell were all his reserves. When they failed he had very little more to say. In his summing up he made what he could of a hopeless case, represented his client as a young gentleman, soberly driving at a moderate speed to his dinner, who was confused by diverse signals shown him by the police. He asked for a nominal fine, if, indeed, his client was to be fined at all. The Assistant Public Prosecutor briefly detailed the proved facts and left the sentence wholly to my discretion.

I gave myself the week-end to think over my judgement. If I fined the accused and compensated the injured women from the fine, I should be on easy ground. Military circles might find the sentence unpalatable, but they would swallow it; nothing more would be heard of the affair in a week. But was that the proper sentence? Suppose one was to turn the case round, suppose the accused was a Burman, a young official who, returning in his car from the Orient Club, where he had been celebrating with his friends, had driven against the red light into a car containing two English ladies with such force as to spin their car across the road, thereby wounding them grievously, what sentence would their outraged fellow countrymen demand, what sentence would the magistrate be likely to inflict? Beyond question it would be a sharp term of imprisonment. Or, if one changed the locale and substituted a road-crossing in England, what would the magistrate do? He too would impose imprisonment, beyond any manner of doubt.

Yet was it possible to pass a sentence of imprisonment on a British Army officer in Burma, even though this was the punishment appropriate to his offence? I was inclined to doubt whether it was possible in a case of the kind before me. I was empowered, of course, to pass the sentence, but I could not see the High Court upholding me on appeal. The Chief Justice, Sir Arthur Page, was on leave at the moment. If he were there, I felt, he would probably uphold me, for he was by repute a man who administered the law without consulting public opinion. But unfortunately he was not there, his place having been taken by one of the puisne judges. Lacking its vigorous head, the High Court lacked the authority to stand up to the executive. Unless I was very much mistaken, the executive was in favour of special treatment for the accused. Though the Government had been careful to give me no hint of its wishes, I knew well enough what certain officers wanted me to do. In their view a fine would be adequate. I knew this because the clubs were ringing with it. It had been reported to me that Mr. McDonnell, surrounded by his supporters in the Gymkhana Club, had said: 'If Collis passes a sentence of imprisonment that will be the end of him.' It was impossible not to draw the conclusion that he believed himself to know the views of the executive, that is to say of those officers who were senior to me in the service and who had the power of showing their displeasure. He was not, I imagine, deliberately conveying to me on behalf of his client a strong hint that it would be the worse for me if I did not make it a fine, because he must have known that I was not amenable to threats. His statement— if he ever made it—is more likely to have been a comment pronounced with the object of calming those of his hearers who had expressed their fear of what I might do.

As these reflections passed through my mind I became convinced that a sentence of imprisonment would not be carried out. The High Court would never withstand the pressure. Even if it did, and I was upheld, the Government had reserve powers. It could release any prisoner on the ground of public expediency. If I sent the accused to jail and the High Court confirmed me, the reserve powers would come into play. The fact was that with Sir Charles Innes and Sir Arthur Page out of the way, the military were too strong for the executive.

Would it not be stupid in these circumstances to pass a sentence of imprisonment? I should be sentencing myself, not the accused. Surely the sensible line was to be actual, to realize what could be done and what could not be done, and to take a feasible course—a stiff fine, compensation, a rebuke? That would content Burmese opinion. The Burmese had been watching the case quietly. The vernacular newspapers reported it at full length. They were satisfied with the way the police had handled the prosecution and they had sufficient confidence in me to take in good part any order I might give. They knew, understood, and sympathized with my predicament and did not demand that I should sacrifice myself.

It was a very tempting course of action. But I could not shut my eyes to the simple truth that a fine alone was not the proper sentence. And I knew that if I inflicted only a fine I should never again be able to hold up my head. I should be doing myself an essential violence. Nothing could mean very much to me afterwards.

Having probed so far, I became as assured as a man becomes who knows himself for a moment, and wrote out the judgement quickly, sentencing Lieutenant Fortescue to three months' imprisonment and a fine of thirty pounds, the fine to be paid in compensation to the two women.

4. THE BALL

The scene in the court next morning was all in character. Lieutenant Fortescue, the centre of this drama of principles, sat beside one of the majors of his regiment. Mr.

McDonnell was close by, wearing the mask of the advocate. I pronounced judgement and sentenced his client.

Mr. McDonnell: 'As your Worship pleases. I am filing an appeal forthwith in the High Court and request that my client may be allowed to remain here until such time during the afternoon as the High Court's orders as to bail are received.'

The court: 'I have no objection, Mr. McDonnell.'

With that I rose and went upstairs to my chamber. Feeling in need of the human touch I rang up Fearnley-Whittingstall.

'Well, it's over.'

'What did you give him?'

'Three months and a fine.'

I could hear a sigh, as if he felt for me. He was a man of great experience. 'That was uncompromising,' he said.

'I couldn't compromise—the law is too important—if you know what I mean.'

'What about golf?'

'Five o'clock, Prome Road.'

During the afternoon word was received from the High Court that Mr. McDonnell's appeal had been admitted and that bail had been granted to Mr. Fortescue pending its disposal, which was fixed for 29 October, a month ahead.

In a week or so the October holidays commenced, and I decided to go up to Maymyo, the official hill-station on the Shan plateau, and stay with Bernard Swithinbank, who at that time was one of the secretaries to the Government. He is now Commissioner of Pegu. Had he then held that charge, what a different story it would have been! I wanted a change of air after my labours; moreover, Swithinbank had arranged to give an exhibition in his house of pictures by a well-known Burmese artist called Ba Nyan, in whose work I had long been interested. The Acting Governor, Sir Joseph Maung Gyi, with his ministers and secretaries, was in residence and most of the senior officials were also on visit. Military society was strongly represented. Indeed, Maymyo was rather a military than a civil station, for it was the headquarters of a general officer commanding.

Thinking more of the exhibition than of the case just over, it did not occur to me that to walk into a military stronghold at the moment when my name was anathema in military circles was a rash and provocative act. I ought, no doubt, to have gone quietly to another hill station and not inflicted my presence upon persons who naturally wanted to enjoy their holidays without the obligation of being civil to me.

However, all this did not cross my mind, and I set out one sultry noon. The train carried me first through a vast sea of rice-fields. The crop was in ear, but was still green, with yellow patches; it stood high and rich, waving in the sun. Two years and three months had passed since I had traversed the plain, coming from Sagaing and full of anticipation. How much had happened in the time! The old monk's prophecy had been fulfilled; the enmity, the notoriety he foretold had arrived. He had reassured me, but I wondered how it would all turn out. I was tired, and though I could not think I should have done otherwise, I wished the business was over and that I might have a rest. Leaning out of the window and letting the air rush past my face I looked over the green towards the blue of the Shan hills. It would be cool up there, I could get back my strength. I had not taken a holiday since I left Sagaing.

Pegu went by, its split pagoda as the earthquake had left it, and soon the sun rolled under the western rim and the colours grew heavy. In the villages near the line one could see girls at the well or carrying home jars of water. It was the immemorial countryside, lovelier for my long residence in the city, the long hours on the bench, the chatter of the clubs.

Night fell and the moon rose from behind the Shan

plateau. We had left the rice-plain and were in a drier zone, which in the moonlight had its own forlorn beauty, with few lights or signs of man's habitation. The train swayed, a slow drowsy train; I lay down and went fast asleep.

Early in the morning we entered Mandalay, which is one of the notable cities of this world. Three thousand five hundred feet above it was my destination, and I had arranged to drive up there by car rather than continue in the train, which climbs the hill too laboriously when one is impatient for fresh air. As we left the station I told the chauffeur to take the road by the moat-side, for I never tired of looking across it to the once royal city. We halted at a white bridge. Some lotus flowers were still out, and beyond them the red walls stretched away towards the hill on which U Khanti, the hermit, lived. The fresh morning air and the dazzling light!—I had forgotten Fortescue, and the mystery of justice, and the conflict in which I was so uncomfortably involved.

After a while I told the chauffeur to go on and we drove down by the south wall, reaching the corner of the moat where Swinhoe once lived, the man whose collection of Burmese antiquities used to delight me when, a junior official, I was stationed at Mandalay. He was dead, his collection scattered to the winds. I remembered his oil-painting of a Mandalay landscape by Dod Proctor. Where had it got to, I wondered; perhaps a Chinaman had it.

The car turned into the twenty-mile stretch which runs, mostly on a high embankment, across the rice-plain to the foot of the hills. Ancient tamarinds threw their inky shade on the white road; and the wind played over the surface of the rice, bending it in waves and tossing the ears like spray.

In three-quarters of an hour the car was on the lower slopes. Here the heat was great, for the sun struck into the gorge. But it was not for long. Soon we reached a zone of teak-trees, and in half an hour were at View Point, two thousand feet up. I stopped the car and got out, to look at the finest prospect in Burma. There is nothing so healing as a long view. From the edge of the road the ground fell away steeply to the plain. In the morning light of that season, when frequent showers had cleared the air of dust, I could see Mandalay, the walls, the moat, even the high finial of Thibaw's palace; beyond curled the river, the great Irrawaddy, on the farther bank of which was Sagaing, with its hills and gleaming monasteries. Looking south over the plain, an immense distance away I could perceive P?pa, the sacred peak, on which still lived, it was said, the Mahagiri spirits which for centuries had watched over the realm.

But it was time to go on and I motioned to the driver. Zig-zagging up by hairpin bends, we came into the zone of oaks. The air was much fresher, one felt an appetite. By easier slopes we reached the village of Anisakan, the Near Camp, where lay old Kierander's strawberry beds, and thence in ten minutes were in Maymyo, driving past the bungalows red with poinsettia. Swithinbank lived in a big house beyond the lake, and I was soon in his porch, shaking him by the hand.

At breakfast he remarked: 'By the way, there's a ball at Government House to-night. We're going and I'd better ring up the Private Secretary and tell him you've arrived.'

'Thanks,' I said. 'I'd like to go very much.'

Presently at the telephone I heard him say: Collis is here and would like an invitation for to-night.'

There was a conversation of some minutes, and when he laid down the receiver, he exclaimed: 'They've invited Fortescue!'

'I didn't know he had come up.'

'Well, apparently he has and they've invited him to the ball!'

'What did the Private Secretary say?'

'He seemed put out, said he had no idea you were to be here.'

'Are they inviting me?'

'Yes, he's sending a card, but he's evidently worried.'

I found the situation extraordinary. Whatever way one looked at it there was no gainsaying that Fortescue had just been convicted of an offence under the criminal law and his appeal was pending before the High Court. An invitation to Government House was surely unusual in the circumstances, unless the Government believed him to be innocent and desired to publish their belief in this way. But before the High Court had spoken it seemed premature to exhibit sympathy, unless they did not mind being accused of seeking to influence the High Court's decision. I said as much to Swithinbank, but he was inclined to think there was no calculation.

'It must have been done by the staff,' he said. 'Fortescue is a friend of theirs. I am sure Sir Joseph had nothing to do with it.'

'Well, I don't care,' I said, 'and I don't suppose that any of the High Court judges who may be present will care. What's the Private Secretary worried about? Does he think I'll make a scene?'

'Perhaps it's the military he thinks will make a scene.'

I could not make head or tail of this. Surely the military had not such a grip that they could dictate who was to be invited to Government House? However, it was clear that nobody wanted me at the ball and the question was whether I should go. At first I decided not to go. I had come up to Maymyo for a rest and it seemed that the atmosphere there was more unrestful than in Rangoon. It was such a small place, too; even if I did not go to the ball I should meet army people in the club or on the golf links. Then there was the exhibition. Everyone had been invited to Swithinbank's house to see the pictures. Clearly, if I did not go to the ball, it would be logical to leave Maymyo at once.

'What do you advise, Bernard?' I asked.

'Oh, come along,' he said, 'it's all nonsense anyway.'

It *was* all nonsense and I decided to go, but I must admit that I had no idea of the strength of the antipathy felt for me by the soldiers. Had I realized that, I wonder whether I should have had the courage to go.

As it was, I set out with Swithinbank and his party, expecting nothing worse than dour looks. Fogarty joined us and other friends, for even in Maymyo there were some people who cordially agreed with me.

In Government House porch I went to shake hands with the Private Secretary. He gave me a scared look when I began to thank him for his invitation. Having little conception of the truth, I tried to show him by my manner that I had no wish to be unpleasant because he had invited Fortescue; but he edged away and began talking to someone else.

We went into the room off the ballroom and the band struck up. I asked a member of our party to dance and soon noticed Fortescue, and also the acting Chief Justice. The comedy of the situation overcame my other feelings and I laughed outright, to the surprise of my partner. But the comedy had a counterpart of which I was ignorant.

Later in the evening, having no partner, I went down the stairs to the refreshment room. At the other end of it were some army officers in mess dress, talking together. When they saw me come in they stopped and stared. I did not know any of them and went up to the buffet, where I ordered a drink and helped myself to sandwiches.

As I ate my sandwiches, I became unpleasantly aware of a tension in the air. At that moment, however, some people I knew came in and I attached myself to them, ordered other drinks, and handed round plates. The soldiers left the refreshment room, which felt less oppressive after they had gone.

Going up again into the ballroom I met a friend and wandered away to the other end of the house. There were

some comfortable chairs in a secluded corner, and there
we stayed, talking. The time flew past, and in the interest
of the conversation I forgot about my party; though what
it was we were talking about I cannot now remember. At
last the band stopped and I could hear cars hooting. I
looked at my watch, saw it was past one o'clock. 'It's all
over,' I said. 'I shall have to explain this to my party as
best I can.'

I hurried into the porch. Swithinbank's car was just
coming up. 'Where on earth have you been all this time?'
shouted Fogarty. I saw some officers looking at me in surprise. But the car was waiting and I jumped in with the rest.

Some days later I discovered the key to these events. I
had occasion to see Mr. Leach, the Chief Secretary, on an
official matter. When the business was over, he said:

'By the way, you have something to thank me for. I
suppose you know that the Camerons are very angry with
you about your order in the recent case.'

'Yes,' I said. 'I have heard something of the sort.'

'The junior officers went to my wife the other day and
said they were going to throw you into the lake. When I
heard about it I sent a message telling them not to be
damned fools.'[1]

'Thank you very much for saving me,' I said. 'That
ought to be a warning to Mr. Justice Cunliffe, who I
understand is taking the appeal, what to expect if he
upholds me.'

At this impertinence Mr. Leach stared very hard and
made it clear that the interview was at an end.

As I returned home I ruminated on what I had just
heard. Certainly it seemed to explain the Private Secretary's trepidation, and my own feeling of 'something in the
air'. Could it have been that towards the end of the dance

---

[1] Indian history here provides a curious parallel. When Lord Ripon
was Viceroy, the mercantile community of Calcutta, enraged by the
Ilbert Bill because it empowered district magistrates to try Europeans,
planned to seize the Viceroy and put him on a ship bound for England.

the Camerons had searched for me in vain? If so, it was a grand joke and the laugh was on them.

I made no inquiries and to this day I do not know the truth about this boyish plot. Nor do I know why they did not afterwards throw me into the lake, for I cannot suppose that they took Mr. Leach's message seriously. Someone told me, however, that they rather admired me for coming up to Maymyo and facing them. After all, they were soldiers and, by birth, gentlemen. But their admiration, if it existed, was misplaced, for the truth was that I never gave them a thought. Even at the ball itself I forgot all about them and sat on in the secluded corner, wholly absorbed in conversation. As it turned out the affair was pure comedy, like a lot else which had happened during the year, but if I had been assaulted it might not have remained at the comic level, for when one is fourteen stone and sound in wind and limb one is not just thrown into a lake.

The exhibition turned out a great success, for a lot of people came and most of the pictures were sold. I did not notice any of the Camerons, but the G.O.C., Major-General Coningham, was there. I went round the exhibits with him and we chatted for some time, for he was somewhat of an authority on oriental art. Presumably he knew generally what was going on, but he showed no hint of it in his manner, which was easy and civil, as if the name of Fortescue had never been uttered. I have had a strong regard for him ever since.

5. THE APPEAL

I was back in Rangoon about the 15th of October. The hearing of the appeal, fixed for the 29th, was eagerly

awaited by everybody. What would Mr. Justice Cunliffe[1]
do? He was a London barrister who had not been in the
East any great length of time, and he had a reputation for
independence, but my view from the first had been that
however right, indeed admirable, my sentence might be
held to be, it could not be given effect in the Burma of
1930. I came to that view because I was sure that the
Government was against anything of the sort, and would,
if necessary, interpose to prevent it. Mr. Justice Cunliffe
was, of course, as well informed on that point as was I.
There were three possibilities. He might agree with me, uphold the sentence, and leave it to the Government to take
what course it considered proper; or he might agree with
the finding, but alter the sentence; or he might disagree
with me and acquit the appellant. The first and third possibilities I considered equally unlikely. As for the second, he
might delete the sentence of imprisonment if he thought it
appropriate to show clemency. I wondered whether the
savage feeling which prevailed had put him in a clement
mood. It would have had the opposite effect on Sir Arthur
Page. But it was no great matter to the accused if Mr.
Justice Cunliffe was not clement, for in that case he could
count on the clemency of the Government. Such was the
position when the appeal was called on the 29th.

I was not present in the High Court, but I read the text
of the judgement next morning in the newspapers. It began
by stating that I had ample evidence to convict and went on
to declare that I was right in having refused to allow the
parties to compound, since it was clearly in the public
interest that a conviction should be registered. Reference
was then made to the question of sobriety. No-one had
testified that the appellant was under the influence of
liquor. I could not find any discussion of the presumption
that he must have been under that influence, failing any
other explanation of his conduct.

[1] Now Sir John Cunliffe, Kt.

Having left the appellant's probable condition undetermined, Mr. Justice Cunliffe then pointed out that imprisonment meant cashiering and he argued that no army officer should be deprived of his career for criminal negligence, however gross.[1] I found it difficult to follow this argument. Could the framers of the Code have intended that the imprisonment prescribed for the offence should be inflicted upon everyone except army officers? Mr. Justice Cunliffe did not say what other class might also hope to enjoy the exemption, but he was careful to explain that by the term 'army officer' he did not mean only English army officers, but included Burman army officers. At that time there was no Burman officer in any regiment of the army.

The judgement concluded: 'I shall cancel the sentence of imprisonment, but as I regard it as a very gross negligence on the part of the appellant I shall impose the maximum fine under the section, that is, I am sorry to say, only Rs. 1,000 [£75]. But the whole of the Rs. 1,000 will be divided equally between the two injured ladies.'

The fine was inadequate, but as imprisonment was impossible it had to do.

In the strait in which he found himself this sentence was the most feasible which Mr. Justice Cunliffe could have devised. It gave the women rather less perhaps than a civil court would have awarded them in damages, but a fairly substantial sum nevertheless, and it made clear that if the appellant had not been an army officer he would have had to go to jail. Since he could not go to jail, it was useless to discuss the presumption against his sobriety; indeed any such discussion might have weakened the necessary conclusion that cashiering was inequitable. Taking it all in all,

[1] This may seem incredible, but the exact words of the judgement read: 'I see no reason why an officer, whether he happens to be a British officer or whether he happens to be a Burman holding the King-Emperor's commission, or whether he happens to be an Indian holding another commission in the army, for a piece of isolated negligence, however gross, ought to be deprived of a useful career in the public service by serving a term of rigorous imprisonment.'

I was very satisfied with the courts; mine had indicated the correct sentence and his had gone as far as the circumstances allowed. It did not seem to me that English justice should suffer in the estimation of the public, while our prestige would stand in consequence as unshaken as it was reputed to stand.

But in this I was in error, for the executive now intervened.

6. THE EXECUTIVE INTERVENES

On 1 November, three days later, I received a note from Mr. Booth Gravely. It was very short, but much to the point. The writer stated that he felt it his duty to let me know, now that the High Court had pronounced judgement, that he had asked the Government to transfer me from my appointment of District Magistrate on the ground of the injudiciousness of my orders in the Fortescue case.

This letter meant that, in Mr. Booth Gravely's view, the fact of my sentencing a British officer to imprisonment in the circumstances described rendered me unfitted to exercise any judicial powers in Rangoon. I decided to protest, because the view was wrong.

Accordingly I wrote to the Private Secretary, asking him to arrange an interview for me with the Acting Governor, because I was doubtful whether I should get much of a hearing from Mr. Leach, the Chief Secretary, or from Mr. Lloyd, the Home Member of Council. I had been to see the latter the day before about the Assistant Government Advocate. That officer had been deputed to appear for the prosecution before Mr. Justice Cunliffe, and in his address to the court had been reported by the newspapers as saying that 'he could not find the evidence going as far as the learned magistrate had allowed himself to conclude and that the highest he could put the case was that the accused had possibly committed a grave error of judgement.' I drew Mr. Lloyd's attention to this and asked him whether the Assistant Government Advocate was speaking under instructions from him. He replied with little suavity that such was the case and that what he had said was in consonance with his instructions. When I pointed out that the Government in that event must have instructed him not to oppose an acquittal he made it clear that he was not prepared to discuss the matter further.

Sir Joseph sent word to say that he would see me at Government House on 3 November at 2.30 p.m. I found him in his office upstairs and got to the point at once by producing Mr. Booth Gravely's letter. He read it with surprise. 'I've heard nothing about this!'

'The proposed transfer', I said, 'is in the nature of a punishment. Are magistrates to be punished by the executive when they pass orders which, though correct in law, are displeasing to the executive?'

'Certainly not,' His Excellency hastened to reply.

'Very well then,' I said, 'I leave the matter in your hands. If this transfer takes place, you will oblige every magistrate in Burma to consult his executive superiors before his conscience.'

'Don't worry,' said Sir Joseph earnestly, 'I'll see to all this.'

'And may I add without offence that if I am transferred on the ground mentioned in Mr. Booth Gravely's letter I shall take the matter to the Secretary of State?'

Sir Joseph looked grave and upset, and again reassured me. Nothing could have been more considerate than his manner. Leaving a memorandum of my complaint I left the room.

On 6 November one of His Excellency's friends came to see me. He said: 'I've a message for you. Sir Joseph says that he may find himself in a ninority in Council, but that he will do the best he can, as he believes you were right.'

When I reflected on this message I perceived that Sir Joseph would be unable to withstand departmental pressure, and I decided to go and see Mr. Leach, the Chief Secretary. His room in the Secretariat was immediately over Mr. Booth Gravely's. I climbed the stairs, sent in my card, and was received at once.

'I have come to ask', I said, 'what you are going to do with me. I suppose you have read the memorandum I left with His Excellency?'

'Yes,' he said. 'I've read it and I didn't like the tone of it, particularly where you said the Government was against the conviction.'

'I said that because the Assistant Government Advocate, as reported in the newspapers, did not support the conviction.'

'I don't know what he said, but I can tell you that the Government was not against the conviction. It was the sentence they objected to.'

'But the sentence was the right sentence.'

'The sentence was the wrong sentence, and it has been put right by the High Court.'

'In that case, what are you going to do?'

'We are going to transfer you; but don't jump down my throat, the transfer will be a promotion. We are going to appoint you to act as Excise Commissioner for four months.'

The appointment of Excise Commissioner was worth £250 a year more than that of District Magistrate.

'And at the end of the four months what are you going to do?' I asked.

'Your leave will be due and I gathered from you on a previous occasion that you wished to take it. On return from leave, of course, you will have a lien on the appointment of Excise Commissioner when it again falls vacant.'

'You must give me a little time to think this over,' I said.

'There's no question of your thinking it over. I have already drafted a letter which is a reply to your memorandum and which contains the orders of your transfer.'

'If there's anything in that letter about injudiciousness in the Fortescue case being the cause of my transfer, I frankly tell you that I'll take it to the Secretary of State.'

Mr. Leach hesitated. 'I shall look through the draft again,' he said. 'In any case it has to be passed by the Governor-in-Council.'

The interview was at an end and I departed in deep thought. I had no power to resist a transfer unless it was ordered for an improper reason, when I could appeal to Whitehall, and I had warned the Chief Secretary that if an improper reason were given I should appeal. This was poor tactics on my part, I knew, but it accorded with my mood, for after all the strain I had gone through I was disinclined for a long drawn-out wrangle. Had I said nothing about appealing to Whitehall and waited till a letter on the lines of Mr. Booth Gravely's was sent to me I could have used it with great effect.

A couple of days later I received the Chief Secretary's letter. It was conciliatory in tone and reiterated what Mr. Leach had already said, that I was mistaken in thinking the Governor-in-Council was against the conviction. The sole objection was the sentence, which if it had been carried out would have meant an end of Mr. Fortescue's career. The letter then disclaimed all responsibility for what Mr. Booth Gravely might have written. Coming to the matter of the transfer, it was stated that I was being posted as officiating Excise Commissioner because it was necessary to find somebody for that post, which had unexpectedly become vacant.

In this way the clash was resolved, a clash of opinion in which both sides believed themselves to be in the right. When people differ as fundamentally as did I in this matter with those colleagues of mine who at the moment were holding the key appointments in the executive, a good course is an arrangement whereby appearances are kept up. The great merit of the Chief Secretary's letter was that it preserved appearances, while achieving its object. I had to be transferred to satisfy a number of people and I had to be promoted to satisfy a number of other people. Those in favour of my sentence included part of the European and, of course, the whole of the Burmese, Indian, and Chinese populations. These people might have shown their resentment with some effect if I had not been promoted, but now their protests, when they made them, fell very flat, and the executive, with their papers in impeccable order, were able to look on with equanimity when the newspapers came out with leading articles.

The articles were numerous, for feeling was strong. Before the transfer was actually gazetted the *Rangoon Daily News*, a newspaper which was not controlled by European commercial interests, protested against it. After making certain flattering references to myself, which need not be reproduced here, it spoke of the necessity of maintaining the high reputation of British justice. 'If British ideals,' it declared, 'have lost much of their original fervour to-day it is because their exponents have not been able to soar above petty inclinations and have wandered away from lofty principles.' Occasionally the public was given proof of British sincerity and goodwill, but the meddling by the executive in the present judicial matter was likely to weaken popular faith in the continued existence of those great qualities which had been displayed by certain distinguished Englishmen in the past.

This protest was followed by many others, as soon as the Government's intentions were officially announced. Even the *Rangoon Times*, a daily supported by the commercial community and in general a staunch upholder of official policy, found it necessary to dissociate itself from the line taken by the executive on this occasion, and in its issue of the 22nd of November made it clear how much the public valued perspective and fairness in the law courts.

There was a good deal more of the same kind; and the Rangoon Bar, as a body, by going out of its way to present the departing magistrate with an address which emphasized what they were pleased to call his impartial administration of justice, showed very clearly its opinion of what had been done.

The officials concerned bore all this without wincing. They were conscientious men who had given up their lives to the administration. They could not have faced what they had had to face during the quarter of a century of their exile unless they had been upheld by an inner conviction of their usefulness and probity. It was this conviction which upheld them now and enabled them to read the newspapers and maintain their aplomb.

I have often wondered what would have happened had Sir Charles been in Burma when this last case of mine was tried. I have never been able to picture him inviting Mr. Fortescue to Government House while the appeal was pending, nor, had I gone to him with Mr. Booth Gravely's letter in my hand, can I think that I should have had the experience which in fact befell me. As for Sir Arthur Page, the Chief Justice, his presence would have insured a passionate resentment of any infringement of the courts' integrity. The way things fell out I had to face alone three senior Indian Civilians who for the moment constituted the Government and whose views profoundly clashed with mine. The Chief Secretaryship might very well have been held by Fogarty, the Commissionership of Pegu by Swithinbank. Had the humanity of the first and the dignity of the second been effectively available, it is inconceivable that the conflict I have described could ever have taken place. But in that event the principle on which I stood would not have been so clearly demonstrated, and at a period when the English throughout Burma were being assailed with accusations of partiality its demonstration was timely, though insufficient to stay the course of events or to deflect the peasantry from the desperate attempt a brief account of which follows in the next section.

7. THE REBELLION

On the 28th of October, the day before Mr. Justice Cunliffe heard the appeal, the man Saya San at 11.33 p.m. caused himself to be proclaimed King of Burma, assuming the title or style of Thupannaka Galon Raja. The coronation took place at the Myasein Taung-yo Pagoda in the Insein district, half an hour's run by car from the High Court. Not a single official heard of it, though it was whispered through the villages of the whole country. The ceremony was carried out in the traditional manner, with the five regalia of the White Umbrella, the Crown of Victory, the Victorious Sword, the Slippers, and the Whisk. On 21 December, a fortnight after my transfer, Thupannaka Galon Raja entered his palace on Alaung-taung Hill in Tharrawaddy, where he breakfasted with his five queens in the presence of his four ministers. Thereafter, seated upon his *Thihathana* throne, beneath which was a lion of banyan wood with ruby eyes, he reviewed his army, four regiments under the command of Thirina-wrata, his general. As they marched past a prayer was chanted: 'May Thupannaka Galon Raja live at Aung Chan Tha, the City of Wealth and Victory, and may his contemplations be speedily successful. May the Guardian Spirits of the Religion, the Dragons and the King of Angels sustain him. May he become Emperor of the Four Islands and of the thousand lesser isles adjacent to them.' At the end of the review a proclamation was read—'In the name of Our Lord and for the Church's greater glory I, Thupannaka Galon Raja, declare war upon the heathen English who have enslaved us.' The army marched away. The rebellion was to begin the following night.

The extraordinary thing about the last paragraph is its truth. All this actually happened on 21 December 1930. Had a London reporter been present that day on Alaungtaung Hill and been told the gist of what was said, it is doubtful whether he would have known what to wire to his paper. Was it a pageant he was witnessing, an historical play, some reconstruction of the twelfth century? Could these people really be thinking of war against an English Government?

But they were. In the words of the official Blue book issued later, the rebellion 'was undoubtedly organized to overthrow the existing Government by force of arms'. That it could have had economic causes was scouted. There was only one motive and one object—hatred of the Government and intention to destroy it. So the Government itself said.

In this connection it is interesting to note that one of the two heads which, it is alleged, the rebels were most anxious to take belonged to Mr. Booth Gravely—an allegation not inconsistent with the Government's estimate of its own unpopularity.

In this matter of heads, however, one should beware of adopting too prosaic an explanation. Besides wanting to indulge their dislike of Mr. Booth Gravely, the rebels had a practical reason—they also wished to make use of his ghost. In Chapter One I gave some information about the constraint of ghosts, how the same might be used to guard treasure. In an earlier book about Burma I described how Tepathin, the ghost of a man who had been put to death to watch a gate, fought for Burma against the Tartars. For all I know Tepathin may originally have been a Tartar.

Certain it is that the rebels intended to constrain Mr. Booth Gravely's ghost to fight for Burma against the English. Mr. Booth Gravely, I am glad to say, is still alive and prosperous, but the rebels, determined to get one Englishman at least to fight for them, killed Mr. Fields-Clarke of the Imperial Forest Service. In subsequent battles between the rebel army and the Government's forces Mr. Fields-Clark's ghost was seen striding in the Burmese van. So a number of Burmans have stated; but some have also said that if they could have taken Mr. Booth Gravely the rebellion would have stood a better chance.

It is curious to reflect that, alive, hatred of oneself may provoke a rebellion which, dead, one's ghost may be seen leading to victory. Really, loyal men should be careful how they adventure into the East!

On 21 December, the very day Thupannaka Galon Raja entered his palace, His Excellency Sir Joseph Maung Gyi held a durbar in Tharrawaddy town, which is situated not far from Alaungtaung Hill. In the course of his speech he informed the assembled peasantry that a petition which they had submitted for reduced taxation could not be granted. Unknown to him there was present in the audience a body of Thupannaka Galon Raja's men who had been deputed to attend the durbar pending the outbreak of the rebellion on the following night. The rebels listened to His Excellency's speech, which hardened their intention to destroy the Government. It is said that Sir Joseph was in grave peril that day. Some of the rebels were for a sudden stroke at him. Had that counsel prevailed he could hardly have escaped, because his guard would have been taken wholly by surprise. Why he was spared is not precisely known; it may have been because he was the first Burman to be Governor.

The next night the rebellion began. As Excise Commissioner my duties lay elsewhere, and I was able to watch its development like an ordinary observer. It provided one of the most extraordinary spectacles of the twentieth century. Though a peasant revolt it was not concerned with obtaining a reform of rural economy, but was wholly political.

The peasants rose because that was their way of expressing the national dislike of a foreign government. Every man and woman in Burma wanted to get rid of the English Government, not because it was oppressive or lacking in good qualities, but because its policy was pro-English instead of being pro-Burman. The educated classes, realizing that they were living in the twentieth century, adopted the tactics which the times offer to unarmed and subject peoples; they presented their claim for a free government to Parliament. The peasantry, whose education was confined to reading, writing, and arithmetic, had no notion what to live in the twentieth century might mean, and having no way, except the traditional way of insurrection, of showing their dissatisfaction, they broke out as best they could. Their best was the best of an age that was gone. The immemorial beliefs of the countryside appeared to them more real than the actualities of 1930.

They had no arms except swords and a few shot guns, mostly home-made. But for them astrology was more actual than armament. Astrologically the end of English rule in Burma was indicated. The science showed that the Burmese would again rule their country about that time. Clearly, therefore, a rebellion was bound to succeed.

It stood to reason, however, that a man with a sword could not ordinarily overcome a man with a rifle, because he could not reach him and use his sword. But since the rebellion was sure of success there must be some way of overcoming that difficulty.

Clearly there was a way. In the East the power of the mind over the body had always been deeply studied. The sages had demonstrated that by meditation the mind could become so powerful that it could preserve the body from ill. It could render the body, as it were, invulnerable. Everybody could not be a sage and command the power which meditation gave, but fortunately there were short cuts. The sages had left prescriptions. The Burmese countryside was rich in these prescriptions. There were medicines. At 11.50 p.m. on the day of his coronation Thupannaka Galon Raja drank such a medicine. And there was tattooing. If certain letters were tattooed on the body the power which those letters symbolized was transferred to the body. By the proper use of pills, oils, chanted formulas, and cabalistic signs, ordinary people could become as strong as sages and be made invulnerable to bullets.[1]

Armed in this manner the rebel bands advanced against the forces of Law and Government.

To show what a fight is like between persons armed with guns and persons armed with magic I shall quote a portion of a court judgement.

'The headman of Shwé-in-don, hearing that a rebel gang had occupied a neighbouring monastery, summoned a party of his villagers, each with a gun, and marched to the monastery. Outside the garden they met a body of thirty men, waving charmed handkerchiefs and swords. Their leaders called out that they must take the guns. After a little while they advanced upon the headman, who retreated towards a banyan-tree. The rebels had one homemade gun and this they discharged, reciting a war slogan. The headman's party returned the fire and killed seven and wounded many others. The rebels, wounded and unwounded, fled into the forest.'

Queer little battles of this kind occurred all over the country. Men advanced upon machine-guns chanting formulas; with amulets in their hands they ran upon regular troops. They pointed their fingers at aeroplanes

[1] Inquiry would probably disclose that the rank and file of both the Chinese and Japanese armies, in spite of their modern equipment, have beliefs of this kind, in a modified form.

and expected to see them fall. They were animated by proclamations such as that issued by the President of the High Missionary Society, a lieutenant of Thupannaka Galon Raja, who had taken the style Dewathila-aung-myayatana, the Holy Lion, the Spirited and Victorious Mya, and who declared: 'Burma is meant only for Burmans, but the heretics took away King Thibaw by force and robbed him of Burma. They have ruined our race and religion and now have the effrontery to call us rebels. The heathen English are the rebels. We have never robbed another's country.' There were men, too, like Shwé Yon, who was known as the Great Doctor. One day he addressed the rebel forces from a dais whereon was a heap of swords, a pile of amulets, and beside him the gong, Aung Maung, the Victorious Gong. He said: 'I now give you amulets which will render you sword- and gun-proof. In the case of this gong, it has magic power. Wish for what you want and sound this gong. When you meet Government troops, sound it and they will be stupefied. Sound it and their arms will flow away like the water of a river; sound it and advance and cut them down.' On the following morning they all assembled at an appointed place, and after having walked round the pagoda three times they marched out under the leadership of Kyabo Tun Maung in the direction of Nyaungwaing. Some of them were in blue-black shirts and shorts. As they marched out Shwé Yon, the Great Doctor, touched them one by one with his finger and gave a style to each, such as Padaweiksa or Thanweiksa (the Flying Man or the Invisible Man) saying that his touch would render them invulnerable. At dawn next day they arrived at Yebya village, where they had breakfast, and on their departure took with them two ten-house ward head-men, who were said to be for the English. 'On our depar-ture from Yebya,' one of the rebels afterwards confessed, 'we came to Kyauk-pon in the forest, where we worshipped a heap of rocks, as it was the abode of a spirit. Then

Kyabo Tun Maung, the leader, tried the two ward head-
men. He said: "These two men are traitors." Having said
this, he addressed some of us thus: "Elders, I turn my
face now." Whereupon Yebo Aung Hmein, his executioner,
killed the two ward headmen.'

To this extraordinary scene Sir Charles Innes hastened
back. Though the rebels had no arms or money and were
certain to be defeated in the end, there was great danger
that the rebellion would first spread from Lower to Upper
Burma, and that the peasantry of the whole province
would be involved. While by no means all the inhabitants
of the affected areas had joined Saya San, there had been
one sinister development. Ex-convicts and other persons
of violent character were encouraged by the general break-
down of law and order to turn bandits, and in gangs which
were hard to distinguish from Saya San's own men began
to prey on the villages and to commit every depredation.
People remembered that at the fall of the Burmese dynasty
in 1885 such bandits had terrorized Upper Burma for
years. If the rebellion spread the bandits would enormously increase and peaceful administration might take
a long time to re-establish.

The key to the situation was the attitude of the legislature. Its members were nearly all men of moderate opinion
who hoped that the neW form of government, which they
wanted just as much as the rebels, could be obtained con-
stitutionally from Parliament. They had not incited the
peasantry to revolt nor did they now lend them any
encouragement. Extreme Left-wing organizations may
have been in touch with the rebel leaders, but none of the
established Burman politicians thought that their country's
freedom could be achieved by rushing unarmed upon
regular troops. As these politicians represented everything
that was modern, educated, and reasonable in Burma, it
was clear that the right course was to get them to London
as soon as possible and there discuss with them in a fair

and open manner the terms of a constitution which should be no less liberal than that offered to India. Such a course would do more than anything else to steady the peasantry.

When Sir Charles Innes returned to Burma early in 1931 such a conference in London had been mooted, but no date had been fixed. The political leaders were suspicious of the Governor's intentions, and when they remembered his draft constitution considered that they had reason to fear a crooked deal. It does not seem that he found time to allay their suspicions and promise them a speedy hearing in London. Instead, he plunged directly into the urgent work of suppressing the rebellion. He obtained troops and aeroplanes from India and his days were occupied in conferences with military and police officers.

I did not think the moment at all opportune to obtrude my personal griefs upon him and I left him in ignorance of what had befallen me during his absence. My resources, mental and physical, had been severely tried, I had had no holiday for three years, for I cannot call my trip to Maymyo a holiday, and a distaste for a system whose passing was marked by the events I have been describing began to torment me. I looked forward eagerly to the arrival of the officer who was to relieve me.

And the East can be too exotic. There comes a time when one longs for buttercups and the hedges of May. I sailed for home on the 30th of April 1931.

8. SETTLEMENT

I was tired when I left Burma, disillusioned and uncertain, but the sea air was a tonic after the Rangoon hot weather and, at large on the ocean, I felt my vitality return and was able to review the events of the previous eighteen months in a mood which became steadily more confident as I drew nearer to England.

The rebellion, which at close quarters had been just another revolt in a year of revolts, now loomed up for what it was, a shocking tragedy. Why had the farmers and field labourers of Lower Burma, peasants whom generationi of English writers had praised for their gentle religion and manners, their charity and high spirits, flung themselves with desperation in front of our machine-guns? For a hundred years they had submitted to our rule, content to call themselves subjects of the English Crown. What had broken their hearts in 1930, making even death seem preferable to longer submission? These were not easy questions to answer, but my experiences had given me some clue to their answer.

It seemed to me that during our occupation of Burma we had done two things there, which we ought not to have done. In spite of declarations to the contrary we had placed English interests first, and we had treated the Burmans not as fellow creatures, but as inferior beings.

Now who were the Burmans, how did they come into our hands?

We took Burma because it was a weak State which could not defend itself and was therefore a danger on our Indian frontier, for if we had not taken it some other European nation would have done so. The Burmese, as a people, had done us no harm, though their court was tiresome and their officials irritating. Major issues of our imperial policy, extending far beyond the merits of the Burmese case, dictated our actions and delivered to us a people of extraordinary charm. Their religion was admirable. They were manly, sportsmen like ourselves; they were artists, amateurs of music and the drama; they were wits, with a vast relish for the ridiculous; they were good-looking and their women, who had rights under their own Buddhist law which Englishwomen have only recently acquired, were beings whose conversation was infinitely diverting. But there was one thing against the Burmans. They were poor. A Burman who had, as many of the villagers had, his own house and his own farmland, a wife and lots of children, a pony and a favourite actress, a bottle of wine and a book of verse, racing bullocks and a carved teak cart, a set of chess and a set of dice, felt himself at the summit of felicity and ignored the English view that he was a poor man because his cash-income was about ten pounds a year. Yet he was poor from the capitalist angle. And, seen from the same angle his country was potentially rich, because it contained large 'resources', oil, silver, tin, and wood, resources which were not being 'exploited'.

Now, as I say, fate handed over to us these Burmans between fifty and a hundred years ago. They were like orphans after the loss of their king; they were children compared to us, because they had fallen behind us in the modern world. But, surely, they were good and interesting material? If we had adopted them as our own, if we had determined to take the place of their king and to be to them everything which an understanding government should be, if we had protected them, brought them up like a father bringing up his sons to take their place in the world, and had acted as trustees for the riches which were hidden in their soil, what a great thing we should have accomplished, how proud we should have been of the modern Burmans, our creation. And the Burmans themselves would have loved us, with a passionate open devotion, which might have made us feel shy, but which would have warmed our ancient hearts. Instead of that, after a hundred years we were mowing them down with machine-guns.

Well, we English are not brutes. If we had not felt that we could adopt the Burmese as our children, spoil them, make much of them, go hungry sometimes so that they could have a good meal, stint ourselves so that they should have plenty, at least we had organized an administration which ensured them peace, order, and justice. We had introduced modern education and built roads; we had provided hospitals and had improved agriculture by irrigation and by a scientific study of crops and soils.

But a great deal of this was nullified by our industrial policy.

The Burmese lacked the capital and the knowledge to develop their mineral and forest wealth. We therefore let in capital from outside. Englishmen, Indians, and Chinese bought concessions and created great industries. The Burmese, of course, shared in the increasing prosperity of the country, because with a greater revenue the Government was able to build roads and hospitals and foster education. The new industries, also, provided much employment. But in the long run it came to this, that nearly all the rich people in the country were foreigners and that the Burmese, from being poor in a poor country, had become the poor in a rich one, a very different state of affairs, which meant that relatively and from every psychological and human point of view they were worse off than they were before. All sorts of foreigners lorded it over them, and had little opinion of them because they were poor.

This is no place to suggest how the Government could have secured to the Burmans a part, at least, of the exploitation of the forest and mineral wealth of their country. It might not have been easy to fit the Burmans for modern commerce and industry, but if they have learned to become judges of the High Court and Members of Council it is fantastic to argue that they could not also have managed commercial undertakings. However, it was much simpler— and, of course, much more directly lucrative for us—to allow private enterprise, in the form of foreign capital, to do the work. This policy created in the long run a situation which was at variance with our best traditions. And it was also a stupid policy, because it rendered the Burmese less competent to undertake the self-government for which it became the object of our administration to fit them. In an earlier chapter I recorded my admiration for two English sailors who saw their native crew into the only boat before they thought of themselves. That is England at its best, that is what deep in ourselves we would like to do always; and it is what, if anything, will enable us to retain our commonwealth and, perhaps, to add to it. But we did not do that in Burma, we did not think of the Burmese first. Many of our Civilians have lived lives of great devotion, have worn themselves out in service to the Burmese. But they could not redress the results of the invasion of foreign capital and of the crowds of Indian labourers who followed in its wake. The Burman became steadily less important industrially in his own country. In the capital, Rangoon, he was nobody. The stigma of poverty beat him down. Government House never thought of patronizing his festivals or his drama, of honouring his monks or— following the Vice-regal analogy in India—of giving its ceremonial some Burmese colour. The merchants treated him like an office boy and the army in its ignorance thought of him only as a happy-go-lucky scamp.

It was all this which was at the back of the peasants' revolt. The situation in 1930 was enough to make any Burman doubt the good intentions of England. The constitutional agitation in India, which at last had obliged Parliament to renew an excellent practice, long discontinued, of getting into direct touch with Indian opinion, had ensured that Indians should get a liberal measure of self-government. But it was unknown whether the Burman would get an analogous grant. It was true that Sir John Simon and his Parliamentarians had visited the country, but their report confined itself to discussing the Indian problem. The rather ambiguous reference to Burma was interpreted to mean that, after separation from the Indian system, Burma would get a constitution, the details of which remained to be worked out. The current belief in Burma was that that constitution would be markedly less advanced than the Indian measure. One of the strongest reasons for that belief was the draft constitution which, as I have said, Sir Charles Innes was drawing up, presumably on instructions from Whitehall, and which in effect would have turned Burma (so it was believed) into a Crown colony, thereby perpetuating the economic subservience of the Burmese people to foreign capitalists.

The Burmese felt that they had not succeeded in capturing the ear of Parliament. The desire of their leaders was to get to London and explain their case, but in 1930 it was uncertain whether a delegation from Burma, representing all interests, would be summoned to London. Impatient, desperate, deluded by prophecy and by the promises of magic, the least instructed part of the electorate broke out.

Before I left Burma in April 1931 various Bunnans of position had said to me: 'You're a man who knows how we stand. This rebellion is a mad affair. Our influence would probably suffice to stop it, if we were able to give assurances to the people that Burma was going to get a fair deal in London. We cannot give such assurances with any prospect of being believed. We don't like to think that Parliament will treat us shabbily, but we've nothing to go on. It is a most awkward position for us. The Government here has told us nothing. We have sent written representations to London without effect. When you're on leave, could you find out what is in the wind?'

'I very much doubt', I said, 'whether anything has been settled. If it had the Governor would have received his instructions and you would have been informed.'

'That is the point,' they said. 'Something must be settled.'

'All I can do is to mention the subject privately.'

During the voyage I thought a good deal about this conversation and wondered what I could do. Certainly it seemed most important to get the moderate and constitutional elements of Burma into touch with the right people in England. On reaching London I went straight to the India Office and sent in my card. The Permanent Under Secretary of State was kind enough to see me and I told him that the Burmans were in a great state of agitation about their fate. The rebellion was a nasty affair and might spread. It would have a good effect to get leading Burmans over to London as soon as possible. The Secretary replied that nothing was yet settled, but that there was a proposal for a Burma conference in September.

I went on to see Geoffrey Faber.

'Back again!' said he, as I was shown in by his secretary.

'I've been away three and a half years, Geoffrey,' I replied, hurt.

'It seems only the other day that we drove down to Oxford in the fog,' said he, offering me a cigarette.

'Well, I'm still in a fog. That's why I've come to see you. A lot has been happening.'

'In Burma?' He was surprised. There is a fiction that nothing ever happens in Burma.

'Yes,' I said, 'in Burma. And I want to talk to you about it.'

'Right, let's go out and have lunch.'

Later, in the smoking-room of the United Universities Club, I told him something of what is written here. He was impressed.

'I think you ought to see Curtis, Lionel Curtis,' he said.

It seemed to me curious that he should name the very man the mention of whose name three and a half years before had been the prelude to all my adventures.

On 4 June I saw Lionel Curtis. Perhaps it was fortunate that I did not fully realize how useful an ally he could be, and I spoke to him as easily as one might speak to a Fellow of All Souls.

'It's like this,' I said, 'if we are going to continue just

shooting down Burmese rustics a gulf will be created between us and the whole Burmese people which will never be bridged in our time.'

'What's your idea?' he asked.

'Bring the Burman leaders over and talk to them. But don't delay.'

'What'll they want?'

'Same as India.'

It took Lionel Curtis about five minutes to satisfy himself.

'I believe you're right,' he concluded, adding: 'we mustn't let Burma drift towards a catastrophe.'

He then told me that he would mention the matter to Malcolm MacDonald, the Premier's son, that very day at luncheon.

As I said good-bye he remarked, smiling:

'Remember, you're an official and Parliament's official source of information about Burma is the India Office.'

'But Parliament sent Sir John Simon to inquire on the spot.'

'Yes, yes. Well, I'm glad you came to me. But don't try and see any politicians or newspaper people.'

The next step was interesting. Miss May Oung arrived from Geneva. She was a Burmese lady, not more than twenty-seven years of age. Her father at one time had been Member of Council in Burma. She had an Oxford degree and had interested herself in the international status of women, being a member of various women's organizations in Burma and India. She was unconnected with politics, though her position in Burma had made her exceptionally well informed of the situation there, while her education and English experience enabled her to express what she knew with clarity. She was practised as a public speaker. In the spring of 1931 she had been deputed to represent the women of the Indian Empire at an international conference at Geneva. It was during a break in the conference that she now visited England. She, also, had been asked to make inquiries in London about Parliament's intentions in regard to Burma.

When I heard of her arrival I asked Lionel Curtis whether he would like to see her. He replied that he would and in due course she called on him. He advised her to go and talk to Malcolm MacDonald, Lady Astor, and Geoffrey Dawson of *The Times,* and gave her the necessary introductions. Lady Astor was interested and arranged for her to address at a luncheon party a number of women of the political world, including Dame Crowdy and Miss Wilkinson. Miss May Oung's address surprised her audience, which had previously been under the mistaken impression that the Burmese would be content with the status of a Crown colony, provided that they were separated from India. Miss Wilkinson and her friends, thinking that Mr. Wedgwood Benn, the Secretary of State for India, might be glad to see Miss May Oung, arranged a meeting between them. He had evidently been giving the subject of Burma some recent attention, for when she asked him whether he proposed to invite the Burmese leaders to London, he replied that that was his intention and that when he made it public he would give assurances at the same time that the future constitution for Burma would be freely discussed with the delegates.

Mr. Benn kept his promise, for on the 21st of August the invitation was published in the terms which he had stated. The conference was to be in November.

Meanwhile the Labour Party went out of power and were succeeded by the National Government, Sir Samuel Hoare becoming Secretary of State for India. This, of course, did not affect the promise which had been given to the Burmese, and their delegation arrived early in November. So favourably had Miss May Oung impressed all those with whom she had come into contact in London that the British Government requested the Governor of Burma to nominate her to the delegation, which he accordingly did.

The Burma Conference resulted in the offer of a constitution to Burma closely analogous to that offered to the whole of India. Discussions both in London and Burma dragged on, during which time the rebellion, which had become largely an affair of bandits, came to an end. When agreement had been reached on the multitude of points which inevitably arise when so large a measure as a new constitution has to be placed on the Statute Book, a Bill was drawn up and passed into law. On 1 April 1937 the Act came into force.

In this manner the Burma which I have described in this book passed away. Though their new constitution does not give the Burmese full control of affairs, there is no doubt that it will enable them gradually to give effect to their wishes. Its successful development, however, will depend not only upon their capacity, but also upon the personality of the governors who may be appointed by the Crown, for it will not be sufficient for future governors merely to stand like watch-dogs and to prevent their ministers from deviating from the constitution. Such a static conception of their duties, however tactfully interpreted, would lead to friction, for the incubus of a negative institution becomes highly irritating. A governor must also stand for something positive, he must stand for those great qualities which I like to think are an essential part of our national character; he must know when and how to put Burmese interests first, and so prove to the Burmese that they are in our hearts as well as in our minds.